Cartooning
Teen Stories

of related interest

The CBT Art Activity Book
100 illustrated handouts for creative therapeutic work
Jennifer Guest
ISBN 978 1 84905 665 6
eISBN 978 1 78450 168 6

The Big Book of Therapeutic Activity Ideas for Children and Teens
Inspiring Arts-Based Activities and Character Education Curricula
Lindsey Joiner
ISBN 978 1 84905 865 0
eISBN 978 0 85700 447 5

The Big Book of EVEN MORE Therapeutic Activity Ideas for Children and Teens
Inspiring Arts-Based Activities and Character Education Curricula
Lindsey Joiner
ISBN 978 1 84905 749 3
eISBN 978 1 78450 196 9

Helping Adolescents and Adults to Build Self-Esteem
A Photocopiable Resource Book
Deborah M. Plummer
ISBN 978 1 84905 425 6
eISBN 978 0 85700 794 0

Teen Anxiety
A CBT and ACT Activity Resource Book for Helping Anxious Adolescents
Raychelle Cassada Lohmann
ISBN 978 1 84905 969 5
eISBN 978 0 85700 859 6

Cartooning
Teen Stories

Using comics to explore key
life issues with young people

JENNY DREW

Jessica Kingsley *Publishers*
London and Philadelphia

First published in 2016
by Jessica Kingsley Publishers
73 Collier Street
London N1 9BE, UK
and
400 Market Street, Suite 400
Philadelphia, PA 19106, USA

www.jkp.com

Library of Congress Cataloging in Publication Data
Drew, Jenny, author.
  Cartooning teen stories : using comics to explore key life issues with young people / Jenny Drew.
     pages cm
  Includes bibliographical references.
  ISBN 978-1-84905-631-1 (alk. paper)
 1. Art therapy for youth. 2. Cartooning. 3. Comic books and teenagers. 4. Comic books and children. I. Title.
  RJ505.A7D74 2016
  615.8'5156083--dc23
                              2015028883

British Library Cataloguing in Publication Data
A CIP catalogue record for this book is available from the British Library

ISBN 978 1 84905 631 1
eISBN 978 1 78450 106 8

Printed and bound in Great Britain

This book is dedicated to Helen, Mum, Dad, Steffy, Granny, Grandad, Nana, Auntie Karen, Maggie, and all the rest of my wonderful family (including Hooter and Cuttlefish), and in loving memory of Wicklea Youth Centre

CONTENTS

Part I Working with Comics and Young People

Part II The Comics

Part III Practical Resources

Lesson Plans and Worksheets

FOREWORD
HOLLY, A YOUNG COLLABORATOR

I met Jenny when I was 13, when she took me and a group of other young people on a weekend away, to train us on how to run workshops about our interests and passions. At the time I wanted to teach others about domestic violence. I have since spoken at and have run workshops at national conferences and organised training for teachers in school. I have taken part in creating resources for teaching about homophobic bullying, sexual bullying, domestic violence, child sexual exploitation, mental health awareness and how to set up an Equalities Team. I have co-facilitated and organised an Equalities Summit and I helped to organise Sir Ian McKellen (Gandalf) to come and run assemblies about homophobic bullying.

A lot of things in my life are reflected in the comics in this book, and I can especially relate to Lauren's story and her battle with Post-Traumatic Stress Disorder (PTSD). The comic has helped me to understand more than I did before; I can see that what I am going through is normal for someone with my condition. The images help the stories to be understood even though they are about complicated topics. When you are reading them it doesn't feel like it was an adult who wrote them, it feels like someone who really understands and is so very passionate about the topics they cover. It is really important for young people to share their stories – it helps other people who are going through the same thing know that they are not alone. Stories about other people have always helped me, because it shows a way out of the situation to a better place.

Sometimes teachers teach things that are not up to date, or they spend way too long on an issue that isn't a problem in their school, while missing out the biggest problem. In my view, children and young people should be involved in creating or reviewing all resources that are used in PSHE (personal, social, health and economic education). These comics are an amazing way to learn and I have really enjoyed working with Jenny on creating the lesson plans. I would recommend them to anyone who is looking for a fun simple lesson that you can do with no experience, that students will enjoy learning and teachers will enjoy teaching.

ACKNOWLEDGEMENTS

I would like to thank the following groups, individuals and friends who have contributed to the authorship of each of the comic stories or inspired/assisted with the work in some way, particularly:

My 'in-house editor' Helen, and Jules Allen and Holly.

To the children and young people I've been working with one-to-one, who have made comics, designed characters and played drawing games with me to help with the ideas for this book.

Groups from Bath and North East Somerset: The Youth Offending Service – especially the Compass Preventions Team, The Young Equalities Group, The Young Carers, The Space Group at Off the Record, Mentoring Plus, St Keyna Primary School and the '10 in 100' Team. Also: Bristol's Freedom Youth, Briony Waite, Kate Murphy, Bradley Edwards, Sonia Mainstone-Cotton, Ruth Sexton, Adam Crockett, Gill Welsh and Henry Ludo. Also, Karrie Fransman, Nicola Streeten, Louise Crosby and Laydeez Do Comics for introducing me to non-superhero comics.

All of the teachers/tutors and fellow learners I met through:
The Institute of the Arts in Therapy and Education, London Art
College, The Arvon Foundation and Bristol Improv Theatre.

My therapists Philippa Vick and Laura Cooper (and Ben Searle!).

DISCLAIMER

I have worked in collaboration with people experiencing the issues in these stories first hand; however, they are not intended to be representative of all groups experiencing similar issues. Not all terms in this book will be acceptable to everyone, but I have tried to remain as inclusive and respectful as possible. No authority on language is intended with these materials.

PART I

WORKING WITH
COMICS AND
YOUNG PEOPLE

INTRODUCTION

Imagine if we could actually see into other people's inner worlds, if we had access to all of their memories and dreams. How differently would we feel towards each other?

We only have our limited language to communicate thoughts and feelings, and we view each other with a level of suspicion and cynicism. We have a tendency to think in black and white, right and wrong, good and bad, healthy and unhealthy. This is a survival instinct, because, in nature, that which is different to us may pose a real threat. This is why our critical thinking skills have become so advanced. Debating skills are taught in schools and role modelled in parliament. Governments communicate with each other by carefully constructing and presenting egos, taking a side, picking each other apart, and jeering and cheering when they succeed in winning an argument.

But we do have an alternative. To seek to understand how we are all connected – all of our experiences and ideas and everything. To challenge each other from a place of compassion rather than attack. By taking the time to understand each others' world views, we could join together our collective creativity and do some things that will change the world.

This struck me one sunny weekend in the Somerset countryside, on a conference with hundreds of teenagers who had been elected to represent young people's views towards a national campaign. Here were young people with the passion and energy to do something brilliant. But while I listened to their discussions, I found I couldn't make out what some of them were there to achieve. I heard one participant say, 'I really want to change something for the better, but I don't think there is anything left to change! Our area is pretty good.'

I thought back to the personalities and the struggles of some other young people I had been working with that year. The person who had grown up in care and had just been institutionalised. The person who had epilepsy, had been relentlessly bullied, and had recently attempted suicide. The person who had been kicked out of home and diagnosed with HIV. I knew that if the young people at this event who felt that there was nothing left to change had met these individuals and got to know them, the spark of frustrated energy I saw in them would be moved to action. If those with the privilege, energy and enthusiasm knew the stories of those seldom-heard young people, they could join forces and become allies in order to really make a difference.

How can we bridge that gap, and facilitate conversation between all young people, regardless of privilege or confidence? One of the buzz phrases you hear at youth work conferences is 'making young people's voices heard'. But many seldom-heard young people don't *know* their own voice. Like all of us, their internal dialogue is mixed up with messages they have introjected from the adults in their lives, their peers and from the media. When I first meet a child one-to-one, often they either tell me what they think I want to hear, or they maintain the monosyllabic 'dunno' position. This is coupled with a cultural habit of disconnecting from their emotions and cutting off from their senses. Many of them tell me they don't have feelings, which isn't surprising when children who have been abused are taught 'anger management', instead of how to notice and give value to the important messages that angry feelings bring.

It's not until they've met a person who can come to meet those difficult feelings, and help them to process them, that their voices become more confident and connected with their experience. If we could help young people to understand their stories, there might be more chance of them utilising a safe platform to use their voices.

An accepted definition of comics is 'sequential art' – the sequence of pictures, words and/or symbols, to convey information, ideas and/or narratives. Art Spiegelman, author of *Maus: A Survivor's Tale* (1986), said 'Comics echo the way the brain works. People think in iconographic images, not in holograms, and people think in bursts of language, not in paragraphs' (Spiegelman 2015). This can take many forms and is not a new way of communicating. The paintings in ancient Egyptian tombs, of sequential drawings and hieroglyphics, are an early form of comic art. Comics are a way of giving others permission to see the 'iconic images' and 'bursts of language' in our minds. To facilitate that is to help others to find their own authentic voices, and communicate that by sharing stories. Imagine if, instead of passively consuming manipulated messages that are fed to them via the media, young people could start to understand their own inner worlds and become authors of their own lives.

If I give a young person a piece of paper and a crayon, whether they produce a scribble, or a drawing of a penis, or a detailed likeness of a dragon, it reflects a part of that person that wants to be seen. Imagine a young person sitting in front of you in a tiny cupboard-turned-office in a school. She will tell you nothing about herself, or her life. You ask her a question and she says 'dunno'. You ask if she minds coming to see you; 'dunno' is her response. This goes on for 30 minutes and it feels hopeless. But you've left a pen and piece of paper on the table, and she starts to doodle. She says nothing about the drawing but leaves it there when she goes. You look at the paper and there is a drawing of a horse. She's said nothing, but *she's let you in on something.*

You might think, she just likes horses or that's the only thing she knows how to draw – it doesn't mean anything. But there is some significance in that horse. If she loves horses she has shown you her passion. If she just knows how to draw horses, there must have been something in her that made her want to invest in only drawing horses over and over again. And whatever the reason, she wanted you to see it. She left it on the table for you to see. The more they are permitted to create, the more of their inner world they express. The shapes, scribbles and images from one session to another begin to form a narrative. The next time, you play a doodle game and she makes another image of a horse. Over time you find out that she loved horses when she was little and that was her safe and happy memory. With these doodles from session to session, she tells you a story. This is an example of comic art – sequential images – by definition.

I never just use comics with young people as my only tool or intervention. Humans are so diverse they need different things at different times. If that style doesn't appeal to that particular young person at that time, we might play the bongos to communicate, or do some life coaching, or play a game instead. But with whatever method it takes to communicate with that person, I've noticed that as they talk or create images or make sounds or build things, from one session to another, their voice can start to come through in other areas of their lives. Over time, alongside all of the other work that goes on – the family mediation, the team around the child meetings – whatever the plan is with that young person, it is as though something shifts. Some of them have ended up creating autobiographical comics, chairing their own meetings, or joining the youth forum.

It can also be something seemingly smaller, but equally as significant. Take, for example, a young man who I will call F. When I first met F he didn't want to tell me much about his life. We went for frozen yoghurt and he sat underneath the table. Session after session went by and he made it clear that he didn't want to reveal much to me. I would bring paper and pens, and he would make a few small doodles and then ask if he could go back to class. Once I brought an old typewriter because I thought the novelty might appeal to him. I was hopeful as he sat still, typing for about 15 minutes. When I looked at what he had written, it simply said, 'aaaaaaaaaaaaaaaaaaaaaa%$£@%*' across the whole page. I might have been disheartened, but I tried to listen to what he was telling me.

I started bringing a sand tray to the sessions. This is a therapeutic tool and there are lots of resources on how to use it (see the activities in the 'Comic engagement' section in Chapter 2). Mine is a tiffin box and I have filled one layer with sand and the other layer with small toys and objects.

A SCENE IN THE SAND

I invite children to play with it as we talk, and sometimes they play scenes out in the sand. Every time, F would find a little brass golden pig and hide it in the sand. Sometimes he would ask me to search for it. We played this game a lot. One day I turned up at his house with my pens and typewriter and invited him to make a comic about the golden pig. He played a few games with me, squirted me with a water pistol and told me to leave. I felt like I hadn't helped him at all, and I was just about to go, when his mum came in and asked if he had told me about what they had been making together. Without me knowing, F and his mum had made a giant golden pig out of papier-mâché and spray paint. His golden pig was beginning to emerge from the sand and out into the world.

THE GOLDEN PIG COMES OUT OF HIDING

It wasn't long after that, that he started to open up. I made a few educated assumptions and showed him a comic I had made about a similar issue to his. He agreed that this was just like his life, and from there he began to be himself more fully with me. He showed his sharp sense of humour, his playful creativity and his intelligence in our sessions. Once we spent the time making up improvised songs – him on vocals and me on guitar. When we finished working together, in his feedback form he wrote, '(the service) is filled to the brim with things! I think we are much happier'.

This is an example of how important it is to be flexible with creative interventions and also to trust the pace that the young person sets. I presented F with activities and experiments, but he chose what level to engage with them. Did he make a coherent and self-aware comic explaining the story of his Golden Pig metaphor, like I'd asked him to? No. What he did create was sequential art, using different types of images, engaging different senses, with different people, about the story of his Golden Pig. And in doing that, he taught me something about the Golden Pig in all of us, who needs to be seen, on our own terms.

A BRIEF CONTEXTUAL HISTORY OF YOUTH WORK AND COMICS

In England, youth work and the policies underlying its practice can be traced back to the 19th century, when there were two main approaches to interaction with young people: philanthropy and activism. The latter involved the practice of cross-generational education and the passing of knowledge between adults and young people. Mutually respectful relationships relied upon getting to know people holistically, in their own life space. Youth clubs were self-governed by members. The adults weren't there to 'fix' the young people, but to share experiences and learn from each other. The purpose of youth work was to encourage leaders of change.

Over the generations, youth work changed shape as the government became more involved. Professionals became increasingly torn between client-centred needs and the priorities of the state. From the 1970s onwards, youth workers' attention was turned towards the 'targeting' of groups that needed 'fixing'. Practitioners were required to label young people and try to change them, within a ticking time limit, to meet someone else's agenda. Services were required to evidence their work through the recording of outcomes, accreditation and targets regarding contact with certain groups. Youth work was to become a means of social control.

I couldn't help but notice similarities when I started to read up on the history of comics. In the 1950s, there was a panic about the perceived negative influence comics were having on children. This led to 'The Comics Code' (Comics Magazine Association of America 1959), which advocated a system of labelling and content regulation. Comics were also to attempt to become a means of social control. They were required to reinforce 'the sanctity of marriage' and were forbidden from stimulating 'lower and baser emotions'. It prohibited comics from encouraging disrespect for established authority by portraying authority figures in an unfavourable light. As a result of this, comics were forced underground. Artists self-published, dodging the rules of the code, giving them the freedom to express and break taboos – in much the same way that youth workers manage to maintain core values despite surrounding external demands.

Now, the popularity of graphic novels and comics has become mainstream, being used even by the medical professions. Ian Williams (2007) set up Graphic Medicine, a website that explores the interaction between the medium of comics and the discourse of healthcare. Comics are being more widely recognised as a powerful medium for understanding our inner processes and the narrative of our experience. They can be subversive, independent and accessible to anyone – you don't need big pots of funding – all that is required is a pencil and a piece of paper.

CHAPTER 1

THE THERAPEUTIC
APPLICATION OF THE ARTS

This isn't a book about how to be an art therapist, but about how to use the activities in this book within the boundaries of your role. If you are a youth worker, comics can be used for informal education and relationship building. Teachers can use comics as part of the curriculum. Mentors can use drawing games to communicate. In the same way that it's useful for anyone working with young people to learn counselling skills, there are certain principles that are taken from a therapeutic approach that I think are important when using creative activities. There are plenty of books and training opportunities to help you find out more about therapeutic approaches, and this book will only touch on some of the basics necessary for working creatively with young people.

The first thing to be aware of is that if a young person creates something, we may not be qualified to analyse or interpret what they have done, but we can be curious. We can help the young person work out what their images mean to them. There are three levels of helping a young person to examine the image that they have made.

1. Describe the image (e.g. 'This is a picture of me standing on top of a mountain').

2. Analyse the image (e.g. 'I think I've drawn myself on top of the mountain because climbing a mountain is a struggle but it's a big achievement, a bit like my life').

3. Be in the image and speak as each of the parts (e.g. 'I am on top of the world! It has been a struggle to get here but I kept going, and now I can see anything and do anything! I am also the mountain: strong, still, not going anywhere').

Sometimes they won't want to comment at all, or very little. There is something very powerful about simply 'bearing witness' to something that a young person has created. They have allowed it to be seen, and you have let them know that you've seen it. Sometimes that is all they need at that moment.

I once worked with a group of young people who were in care. We were sitting on the floor and playing with a box of art materials. One boy had found a blank mask and was decorating it with drips of red paint coming from the nose and mouth. He'd coloured around one of the eyes in dark blue/green. On the forehead he'd stuck a goggly eye. I asked him what he was making. 'Dunno, just a mask thing,' he replied. I commented on the red and the dark circle around the eye. 'Yeah, he's been in a fight. He's got a black eye and a bleeding nose. He thinks he's a gangster.' I noticed the third eye on the head. 'Yeah he's got a third eye! Because he's seen a lot! He's been through a lot!' I asked if it reminded him of anyone. 'Nah, are you trying to say it's me? Nah. It's just some bloke who thinks he's a gangster.' That is the extent to which he was willing to analyse his image, but it felt like he had shown me a lot of himself during that session.

If they are willing to talk about their creations, to learn more you can ask questions such as, 'Which bit of the picture would you like to talk about first?' 'Tell me a story about what is going on in the picture.' 'Can you give the picture a title?' This isn't a therapeutic technique but if they are hesitant, I sometimes suggest we play a game — which involves us each taking turns to say a word until we have told the story. If we do this, I try not to use 'game changer' words, but stick to the facts of what I can see, or use connecting words so that the child is in control of the direction of the story. For example:

Me: The

Child: Ship

Me: Is

Child: Sinking

We keep this up until we have a full story about what is going on.

To explore other levels we can ask questions such as, 'What does this part of the picture want/need?' 'What does it want to say?' 'Can you try speaking as if you were that part of the picture?' Creative enquiry is reliant upon good intuition about what is safe to ask and also when to stop, and being aware of the boundaries of your role.

IMPROVISATION

Experience has shown me that plans almost never go as you expect them to when working with young people. Human interactions are not predictable. Improvisation involves making something up in the moment, before you have time to think, and is known as a method of acting or comedy for the entertainment of an audience. It can also be seen as a tool for life — for communicating and unleashing spontaneous creativity. It has helped me to learn specific improvisation techniques.

The first rule of improvisation is SAY YES. When a child defines something they have drawn or made, this means you agree. So if a child says, 'I have drawn a gangster' and you say, 'He doesn't look like a gangster — looks more like a zombie', it puts a stopper on the process and takes away from the child the right to define what they have created. If they say the yellow blob is a self-portrait – don't argue with them but accept it as is.

Another improvisation technique is not only to say yes, but YES, AND. This is about your contribution to the scenario. The way I've interpreted this rule into my creative exchanges is to offer an option of continuity. So rather than do one thing and then go on to something else straight away, I try to think of ways to build on the child's original creation. Someone I am working with made a comic about a gold digging fairy called Liberty. The comic took about six months to make alongside all of the other things we were doing, but when it was finished I could see that there was more to do with Liberty. The story was reflecting whatever we happened to be exploring about their life at that time. So the next session we played another engagement game with Liberty at the centre of the action. I asked them to draw Liberty on a large piece of paper and we played 'one-minute-pass-it-on' (see 'Comic engagement' section in Chapter 2). Liberty becomes the transitional figure and acts out different stories and different moods, reflecting the young person's inner world each time I see them.

LIBERTY THE GOLD DIGGER

'Mistakes' are opportunities. The child I mentioned said that they'd made a mistake drawing Liberty's eyes. Instead of ripping it up and starting again, I asked if we could turn the mistake into something new. As a result, Liberty wore sunglasses throughout the story. It's a quirky contribution to the shady 'mask' that the character portrays.

It stunts creativity if we are worried about perfect creation. Many comics and zines include crossings out and scribbly mistakes – it gives them realness. Imagine how liberating it is for young people who are under constant pressure to get good grades, to be given not only permission, but encouragement to make mistakes. We need to have a positive attitude towards mistakes and to the vast learning we can gain from them. Embrace them in comics where possible.

UNDERSTANDING COMICS

Scott McCloud – author of the important titles *Understanding Comics* (1993) and *Reinventing Comics* (2000) – has reflected on something that I have learned in my therapeutic training. That is, we project our inner world onto blank spaces and blank faces, and this is maybe why comics appeal to us. If we see a photograph of a person, our brain lets us know that this is someone who is 'other' than us. We don't empathise so much with a photo as we do with a minimalist cartoon face with two dots as eyes and a line as a mouth, such as Charlie Brown. McCloud theorises that maybe the reason for this is because when we are in a conversation with someone else, we have a very clear image in our head of what they look like, because we are looking at them. Unless we are looking in a mirror or at a photograph of ourselves, we don't have that clear a picture in our minds about what we look like. We have a vague sense of where our eyes and our mouth are – a vague sense that places itself as two dots and a line. So when we look at a cartoon face, that face replicates what we are sensing of our own face – *that could be me.*

TWO DOTS AND A LINE

Cartoons relate to our nature rather than our nurture. We are *programmed* to search for faces and read them in a way for survival. We aren't biologically wired to search for words and read them – we are *taught* to read, and some only learn limited literacy. If you are lost in a forest, surrounded by darkness, but a face is lurking between the bushes – you are wired to zoom into that face and read it for signs of it being friend or foe. Then we can respond quickly enough to go into fight, flight or freeze and save ourselves if necessary. This is why we see faces in everything – if something is placed to look a little like eyes and a mouth, we will see a face. Because of this, it is easy to create characters that appeal to anyone regardless of age or what language they speak, and you can do it with just two dots and a line for a face – no artistic skill required.

Last, a theory that is useful when understanding stories is Transactional Analysis and the idea that we develop 'life scripts' (Berne 1961). Throughout childhood we are perceiving and retaining information from the outside world, whether those messages are delivered to us intentionally or not. We decide what behaviour will deliver us the best chance of safety and approval and we begin to make internal, subconscious rules to follow. If something is repeated to us, it becomes part of our 'life script'. A child might have formed a script very early on that tells them that adults can't be trusted to respond to them emotionally, therefore emotions should be hidden. For example, if a parent leaves, and the other parent can't regulate their own emotions, the child will hide their feelings away. Later, if their youth worker cancels an appointment due to illness, the child takes that as proof that adults can't be trusted. They will gravitate towards people who reinforce this belief. Scripts can always be justified or broken – the trouble is, we are constantly looking for evidence to justify them to prove that our survival technique is correct. This is why we live out patterns over and over again. As Freud (1909) said, 'Something which has not been understood inevitably reappears, like an unlaid ghost, it cannot rest until the mystery has been solved and the spell broken.'

In Gestalt theory (Perls 1969), the messages we 'swallow whole' from the outside world and live our lives by are called introjects. Over the page is a comic I made to help explain the idea of introjects.

We can't swiftly change someone's script with a brash or clumsily challenging intervention. It is like pulling away the person's entire system of beliefs about the world, and you will be met with resistance. I use comics and stories alongside careful interventions over a period of time, which gently offer alternatives to their script. If a child has the 'don't trust' script, I hold that in my awareness while we are working together, and I look for opportunities to explore it with a story that relates somehow to them. Stories aren't threatening because they aren't directly about that person – they are a step away from them. What is even more powerful is if you can allow other young people to share stories, they can gradually challenge each others' script patterns. One young person gave me a card when I had finished working with her that said 'you have made me realise that maybe not all adults are as bad as I thought'. That is the feedback that I value the most above hard outcomes such as getting a job; although that is important, it is the script messages that will have the longest lasting impact on a person's life.

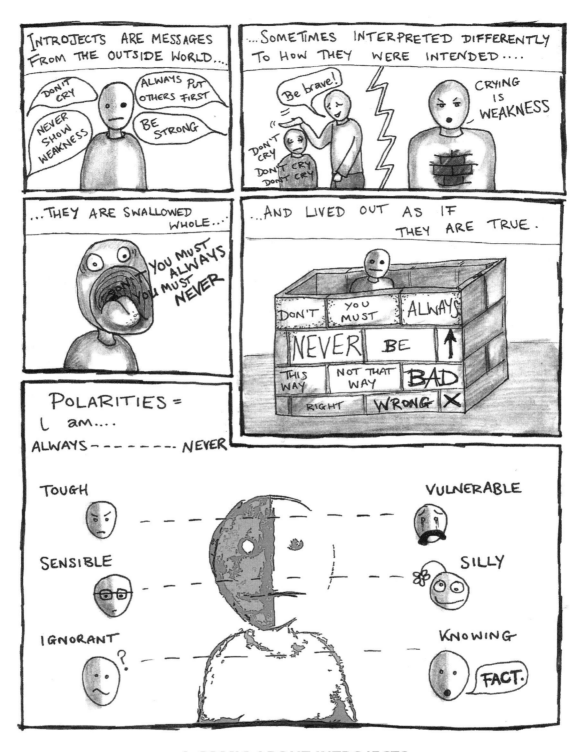

A COMIC ABOUT INTROJECTS

THE COMIC
PARTICIPATION MODEL

The Comic Participation Model is something I have drawn up to help myself to design interventions when I am asked to do creative work with young people.

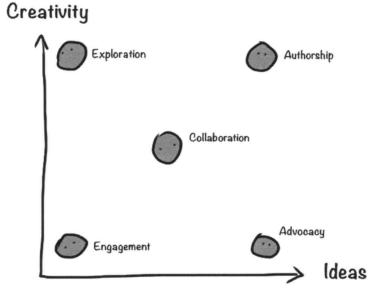

THE COMIC PARTICIPATION MODEL

As you can see in the diagram, there is an axis labelled 'creativity' and one labelled 'ideas'. Both of these indicate a spectrum. This is not to assume that some people are creative and some aren't, that some people are 'ideas people' and some aren't. Everyone has the capacity for creativity and for generating ideas. However, depending on contextual circumstances, how accessible that creativity and those ideas are to them can vary.

Here are some examples of why someone might be low on creativity or ideas at the time you come to work with them:

- They may be holding resistance about creativity and imagination, based on their own life script patterns. They might have been teased or criticised in the past, or have grown up in an environment that doesn't allow freedom of expression.

- They might be low on resilience and creative energy due to their mental health or personal circumstances at that time. They might be too exhausted to create and imagine, even if they are 'creative types'.

You will be able to identify other barriers to creativity and imagination. It is important to give this some thought when designing your intervention. When you meet the group or learn about them for the first time, try to get some idea of where they might be on the scale, and be prepared to amend your intervention.

You also need to be aware of what the desired objective or outcome is of the project.

- To create something attractive and polished for a logo, website or magazine?

- To encourage expression of creativity and the generation of ideas?

- To build relationships?

- To tell a story or communicate a message to an audience?

The next sections will describe some interventions for exploration, engagement, advocacy, collaboration and authorship, with specific examples of how I have used them and why.

COMIC EXPLORATION

AN EXPLORATION SESSION

This is when creativity is high but ideas are low. In this instance you could bring a selection of relevant graphic novels or images for inspiration. Alternatively, you could print example comics from the internet. Find out what they like about the different styles.

Help them to make a mind-map of possible ideas. In the middle of a blank sheet of paper, write your theme. Circle it. Now, spreading outwards, write different aspects of your theme. You could call them subtopics. They can include drawn images or printed pictures to accompany ideas. Then think of personal stories relating to these topics and note them down or doodle them.

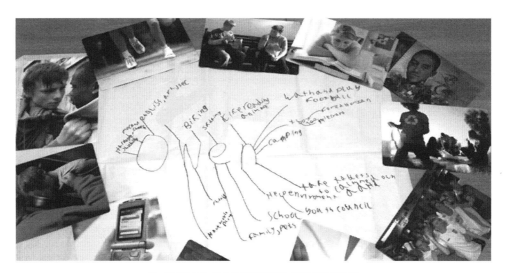

A MIND-MAPPING SESSION

Comic engagement activities will also help to unblock ideas through free association and goal-less artwork.

COMIC ENGAGEMENT

I use these activities with groups or individuals to experiment, to build rapport and dissolve insecurities and resistance about being creative. They require little artistic skill and are mostly improvised. They can also be used as warm ups to more outcome-focussed creative projects, as icebreakers, team building activities, one-to-one work and work with families. I always carry with me a pencil case full of coloured markers, crayons and a pad of paper, in case it seems appropriate or useful to play one of these games. They are useful when you need to access the playful parts of the brain in order to feel safe and to connect (for an explanation of the different parts of the brain, see Lauren's story in Part II). I often use them with children while we are sitting around nervously waiting for a meeting to start.

Some of these activities I have made up, and some I have borrowed or adapted from activities I've seen others use.

◼◼◼ MAKE YOUR MARK

Purpose: Letting go of control, resistance, freedom to make a mess, expressing emotion, getting over the fear of a blank page, accessing different parts of your brain. Nobody has to feel self-conscious about artistic ability.

Materials: A giant sheet of paper – newsprint, flip-chart or sugar paper. The best drawing materials for this activity are messy – something like pastels, chalk or charcoal.

Instructions: Pick something to draw with and start to make marks on the paper – don't worry about what they look like. Then try making marks with your eyes shut. Make marks with your non-dominant hand. Make marks with your non-dominant hand and your eyes shut. Make slow marks. Make fast marks. Make marks that are angry, sad, joyful, shy, boisterous, confident, jealous, bored, excited, calm, safe...

Discuss what that activity was like. Did you enjoy it? How easy or hard was it to access emotions and translate them into marks?

Tips for facilitator: Use your intuition when deciding how long to wait in between instructions, and try adding in your own adjectives. Include some contrasts – going from angry to calm. End the activity on a peaceful note. Some people's emotions are very close to the surface whereas some are less accessible. Be curious about how participants found the activity. You need to rely on your skills as a facilitator to keep the group safe.

FUNNY PORTRAITS

A PORTRAIT OF THE AUTHOR

Purpose: To make eye contact, relationship building, building trust, having fun, letting go of defences.

Instructions: Draw each other without looking down at the paper.

Tips for facilitator: Eye contact is not ok for everyone – due to cultural, physiological, emotional and other kinds of differences. Be sensitive to this, and don't do this activity if you have doubts about how the child will respond. It should be a fun activity and you can have a laugh with each other about the unflattering results.

▪▪▪ HEADS, BODIES AND LEGS (EXQUISITE CORPSE)

Purpose: To have fun, relationship building, creating something unique together.

Instructions: You can play this with two players or more. Without looking at what each other is doing, draw a head in the top third of a strip of paper and then fold it over with just the end of the neck showing. Swap the paper over and then each person, on their new piece of paper, draws the trunk of the body in the mid section, leaving a third of the paper blank at the bottom. Again fold over the section you've drawn so that the next person you give it to can just see the lines of where the body ends and the legs will begin. Last, draw the legs on the swapped pieces of paper. When you unfold the paper you will have a strange mix of drawings that make up a full body.

Tips for facilitator: This game is fun because it doesn't matter about drawing skills – the creature will look bizarre with the mix of styles. It can introduce the idea of collaboration because you are creating something unique together. Sometimes the characters created are so impressive we make comics, starring them in the lead role.

▉▉ DOODLE COLLABORATION

Purpose: Relationship building, non-verbal communication, the potential of collaboration, 'turning nothing into something'.

Instructions: Each person folds a piece of paper into six squares. On each square make a mark or a scribble until each person has six scribbles. Then swap the pieces of paper with someone and spend one minute turning the scribbles into a picture. Choose your favourite creation and tell your partner and/or the others in the room what you like about it.

Tips for facilitator: This is a really good way of breaking down barriers between people who have just met, and is a good alternative to spoken icebreakers. It can be easier to connect initially on a non-verbal level, such as with this activity, and once people swap back the paper there is often a surge of enthusiastic chatter.

▰▰ ONE-PAGE STORY

Purpose: To bond as a group, to explore dynamics, to create something together, to encourage spontaneity.

Instructions: Each person has one minute in silence to draw something on a piece of paper. They then pass it to the next person who also has a minute to contribute something to the picture. You keep going for as long as you want. The group then comes up with a title for it and tells a story about what is happening in the image.

Tips for facilitator: You can learn a lot from the discussion afterwards about dynamics within the group and if they are reflected in the story. There may be mirrored themes that come up. Find out how each member felt when it was their turn to draw – what was it like to have the attention on them? How did it feel having to let go of control to the rest of the group? This activity can also be used with families or staff teams.

▰▰ IMPROV COMIC

Purpose: Relationship building, non-verbal communication, mirroring, paying attention to each other, encouraging spontaneity, humour and creative flow.

Instructions: Do this activity without talking. One person starts by drawing a cartoon panel with the first element, maybe a character with a speech bubble. The next person draws the next element in the box – it could be another character joining in the conversation, or an object, or the environment. Continue this method of improvised drawing until you have a whole comic page or strip.

Tips for facilitator: This is better with people who already have some level of trust and a relationship. Suggest at the beginning that if one person is confident drawing and the other isn't, maybe one could do the drawing and the other do the writing – but emphasise that this is a non-verbal activity so verbal negotiation should be avoided.

■■■ HOW IT HAPPENED STRIPS

Purpose: To break down the events of something that has happened and to reflect on it.

Materials: Post-it notes and pens.

Instructions: Use Post-it notes as comic strip boxes. Describe an event from moment to moment by drawing stick people, basic shapes and/or speech bubbles on Post-it notes. Arrange them in the correct order of what happened by sticking them to the table. Once you have ascertained the story, you can move them around or draw alternative scenes to reflect on what you could have done differently and how that might have changed the story.

Tips for facilitator: This activity can help children who find it difficult to recall and articulate events, and to engage the visual and kinaesthetic senses as well as the auditory. It is easier to remember details of events when they are pieced together as a series of visual images, and to be able to see alternative possibilities at each moment.

TRUMPS

Purpose: To make a visual representation of the people in your life, and what their roles are.

Materials: Blank playing cards (you can buy online or at art and craft shops), permanent markers (I use Sharpies), Top Trumps cards (you can buy in toy shops).

Instructions: Top Trumps is a card game you can buy in most toy shops. Each pack is based on a theme, such as comic book heroes or characters from a popular film. Each card in the pack shows a list of scores for different attributes. For example, the scores may include strength, power or intelligence. I quite often go to the shop with a child and let them pick a pack based on what they're interested in.

Choose a trump card to represent each member of your family, or friends, or the people in your life supporting you (social worker, teacher, etc.). You can use the trump cards alongside some of the worksheets in Part III, such as arranging them into the circle of support.

Tips for facilitators: I use the trump cards to find out more about the child and their lives – which is your favourite character, what do you admire about them? Which character has similar qualities to you? I sometimes encourage the child to make their own cards. This is particularly useful to make sense of the professionals involved in their support plans. The child draws each person and then fills in categories such as:

Who? My counsellor

Where? At school

Why? To talk about my feelings

How? Talking, drawing, sand trays

The child can keep these as a reminder. There is one young man I work with who keeps all the cards we've made in a collections folder.

COMIC ADVOCACY

Comic advocacy is something I use to describe the kind of work that involves me creating visual art to communicate young people's words and stories, either on their behalf or to explore an idea or story with them. I've used this approach for different reasons, mostly based on the objectives of the project. If the objective is to convey a message or a story in comic format, and the young people aren't able, for whatever reason, to create it themselves, then I use this approach. I also sometimes use this as a tool when I want to share a story with a young person to educate or mirror something back to them.

This approach is for those professionals or artists working with young people who have the time and confidence to produce comic style art. Having said that, you don't need to be a very advanced artist – most of what I've learned to draw is by illustrating the stories in this book. All of the comics in this book are examples of advocacy. Active listening is very important with this style of intervention, as you want to portray effectively what young people have communicated to you. I will explain how each of the stories demonstrate examples.

Allen

I made the Allen story with the local Young Carers art group. They had been engaged in creative projects with supportive professionals and had invited me to the group so that they could be involved in the development of the story and the character. I wanted to communicate the therapeutic benefits of making stories about life experiences. I brought a selection of existing autobiographical graphic novels such as *Lighter than My Shadow* by Katie Green (2013), which is an autobiography about the author's experience of having an eating disorder, and *Billy, Me and You* by Nicola Streeten (2011), which is an autobiography of one woman's grief about losing her child. I also told my own story of being a young carer, which I'd made into a comic while on my art therapy course. They then came up with the idea of the character, his personality and his story. They designed his look and mind-mapped his story by answering the following questions:

- Who does the character live with?

- Who does the character care for and what does that involve?

- How self-confident is the character?

- What would most upset this character?

- Is the character an introvert or extrovert?

- How does the character deal with

  » anger?

- » sadness?

- » conflict?

- » loss?

- What does the character want out of life?

- What would the character change about his or her life?

- What motivates the character?

- What frightens the character?

- What makes the character happy?

It was during this workshop that I realised how important it is to create a safe environment while sharing stories. A few of the young people were touched emotionally in ways that I wasn't expecting — there were tears and a lot of emotional regulation needed from the youth workers. Afterwards the staff gave me feedback that they also weren't prepared for that reaction, as this group were usually very contained. I know that these young people had a lot of support and help to process what had come up. However, stories can trigger emotions and memories — which makes them a powerful tool — but we must prepare young people for that. For guidance about this, see the YESS plan, as described in 'The Safe Spoken Word' in Part III.

Brian

I first created the Brian story to communicate with a few of the young people I was working with who happened to have ADHD. I needed to explain the process of how I would work with them — the referral, building a relationship, writing an assessment, the 'Team Around the Child' meeting, and the planning process. I wanted to explain this in a way that they could easily understand and feel involved in.

After I had made the first few pages, I took it to show one of them. He read it and said, 'I really like this — that's exactly what my life is like.' When I asked if he had any ideas for the rest of it, he came up with all of the suggestions that I used for the final draft. He stopped referring to the character as Brian and started to talk in the first person — like he'd forgotten we were talking about a character and were now just talking about him. He was so engaged with the idea that I was creating something about him, it was as though he had just then started to believe I wanted to hear what he had to say. I'd found a way to engage a boy who previously wouldn't sit down with me and talk about himself for more than a few minutes, and not only that, he was proactively planning his own Team Around the Child meeting and work plan — which is the exact kind of child-centred work that we strive for.

Emily

I conducted this session in much the same way as I did with the Allen story, with the local LGBT youth group, but the response was not as emotionally charged as it was with the Young Carers group. I prepared them beforehand for the content of my story about being a young carer, and I imagine that it was less triggering, as the issues weren't as close to home for these young people.

Jay

The character Jay was loosely based on a young person I worked with, and through advice and discussion with the Bristol LGBT group, Freedom Youth, I developed the content for the comic. I found that there was so much information and variation in the life stories of the people in the group, it didn't seem that one story could demonstrate all of the issues. I tried to include a number of the characters' dialogue using quotes from our discussions. One young person pulled me aside just as I was about to leave after a long discussion about gender and said, 'I think it's important to say in your comic that there is no right or wrong way to experience gender. Labels can be helpful but ultimately it is about being yourself.' This is the final thing Jay says on the last page of the comic while he is walking through a rugby stadium with his younger self, hand in hand.

Lauren

Lauren is based on a number of inspirational young people I've worked with. I mainly devised the story with one young man who took part in training professionals, by sharing his life experiences and how he'd been helped by a mentor. He told me about what it's like to deliver public talks about his abusive past, and about how that can occasionally bring back triggering memories. He had suffered the thoughtless comment of an internet troll when his video went viral, and it struck me that this was something that had stuck in his memory, despite the many positive comments. We talked about how he used art therapeutically, and how he's gone on to help other young people.

I devised the YESS plan in consultation with young people, after having my own negative experience of publicly sharing a personal story, and the emotional repercussions of that. I find that a level of self-disclosure tends to happen when working with stories. We learn a lot from each other when we share and compare experiences. Rather than 'off loading' to those I work with, I am mindful of my intentions. If used in the right way, I believe self-disclosure can bring a level of respect and honesty to the relationship, and give permission for others to share more of themselves. This is when true cross-generational passing of knowledge and experience can become a collaboration in creating something new.

Work with Child and Adolescent Mental Health Services (CAMHS)

Described by the young people of Swindon, Wiltshire & B&NES CAMHS participation team.

These are comic pages I made in collaboration with the Oxford Health CAMHS participation group for their website (2015). We had five sessions – starting with a creative session of games, looking at how comics work and mind-mapping ideas. We then looked at different graphic novels and comics that are available – they particularly liked Katie Green's *Lighter than My Shadow* (2013). We discussed how she'd portrayed the eating disorder as a black scribble, following her at different times throughout the book, taking on different shapes and sizes. The next sessions they thought about each of the conditions using a stack of postcards featuring a range of styles of artwork and images.

They each picked a selection of cards they felt represented something about that mental health issue. For example, while thinking about panic attacks they chose the image of a train. They described the feeling of having a panic attack as similar to being stuck on a train – moving at great speed but not being able to move or escape. The postcard method of generating ideas works well because young people can be creative without needing to have any artistic ability at all.

COMIC COLLABORATION

Collaboration involves two or more people working together to add value to the project – whether that be to enhance the relationship between the individuals involved, or to bring something extra to the creation. On the model of comic participation I have placed it right in the middle of the scales, to indicate that collaboration should be used to enhance ideas and creativity. There are examples of collaboration in this book. Another example I haven't mentioned is when a young person's drawing is enhanced to make the lines more confident and the colours more vibrant, while not altering the essence of the original artwork. It helps to have access to, and a level of competence with, digital image editing software, but if that's not possible simply going over the drawing with a fine liner may have enough of a desired effect. I integrated this into a project I did with a group of primary school children, which I will describe below.

There is a time and a place for this approach and it probably isn't in therapy. However, for specific types of projects I think this approach is great for:

- showing the child the potential of their work. If you have confidence with your style, it can make up for technical ability. Many grown-up artists strive to get that childlike look of spontaneous honesty. Take for example the artist David Shrigley (www.davidshrigley.com). You could mistake his style at first glance as being the work of a child – it is simple, profound and funny

- creating something with a quality that could be used on a website, leaflet or book. A pencil drawing with faded pencil crayons won't be useable for a website, but the essence of the drawing can be preserved with a bit of work by an artist.

'My Magic Path' is a programme I developed that allows children to use storytelling and art materials to explore their inner world, express difficult emotions and overcome problems through metaphor. They project onto objects in a sand tray, and develop them into fictional stories. They choose a character and explore the different aspects of that character and its world, identifying the challenges that they face, and helping the character to overcome them in a story. The children narrated while they played, and I took careful notes. They sketched what they had created in the sand and I took their sketches home, made them bright and polished and added them to the text of their story that I had written up. They were aware that I was going to do this and they were excited about it. They bombarded me with instructions such as, 'Can you make her dress bright pink?' 'Can you make the rocket be flying across a starry sky?' My intention was to portray as accurately as possible what they visualised in their heads, using their instructions and sketches. They were given their bound storybooks at the end of the programme. Teaching staff gave the following feedback:

Some of the children whom I have worked with before have not shown the ability to create a story with a beginning, middle and end – the sessions demonstrated that they all had this ability. I saw children who find it hard to be positive about themselves and others become more confident about their own abilities. They were all very proud of the story they produced and also praised the others. Excellent programme and extremely beneficial. The ideas would be useful to be used in the wider school community for children who find it difficult to write stories or express their emotions.

COMIC AUTHORSHIP

Authorship happens when the young person realises their ideas and narratives and puts them onto paper as sequential images with their own words. It isn't enough to assume all young people can do this without support and direction, however. When I compiled a zine, made by young people, I did not receive one comic as a result of the 'call for submissions' poster that I sent out to youth clubs and schools. All of them came on the back of a workshop or support by a professional that I had trained in the art of comic making. Here is how we did it.

We started with a flyer and call for submissions for 'Atomic Comic' to all Children's Services and external partners, but I knew that wouldn't be enough. We needed a team of professionals who understood the importance of sharing stories and were prepared to help to guide young people in creating submissions. We ran a workshop for professionals, covering engagement activities, storytelling, the theories about the therapeutic use of comic making, and a funny and moving performance from autobiographical comic maker Andrew Godfrey about his experience of having cystic fibrosis. The day finished off with each professional creating their own comic.

The course was attended by a range of professionals from services such as the Youth Service, SARI (Stand Against Racism & Inequality), CAMHS (Child and Adolescent Mental Health Services), the Youth Offending Service, Social Care and local charities.

We produced a toolkit for each participant including a hand-made zine style booklet featuring activities from the day. The head of service said that this workshop received the best feedback she had ever seen from a training day. For a plan of how to run this day in your authority or with your young people, see 'The Safe Spoken Word' in Part III.

PART II

THE COMICS

HOW TO USE THE
COMICS IN THIS BOOK

There are five comics covering the following topics: Young Carers, ADHD, LGB and Homophobia, Gender, Trauma and Resilience. The final comic, Cartoon Your Life, is a fun comic about how to make your own comics. It can be used as a stand-alone activity or as part of a longer scheme of work using comics. It is intended to explain the basics of comic making and encourage free expression, rather than focusing on artistic ability, so it should be accessible for most people. This is covered in more detail in Part III.

Each of the five stories comes with a lesson plan and worksheets. They are designed for use as part of a PSHE programme, but they can be used in other contexts. You might stick to the plan, or you might choose sections that are appropriate to those you are working with. There are a few things that I recommend you always do within these sessions.

1. Prepare and do your own research beforehand. Topics such as gender and trauma are complex and should be delivered with confidence. I'm guilty of 'winging' sessions now and again (I'm a better improviser than I am a planner) but only if I am confident in my own understanding of the subject. Ask someone else to deliver the session if you don't feel able to.

2. Some of these lessons may bring up issues that leave you feeling personally vulnerable or exposed. When you are preparing for the session, question, is it emotionally safe for me to deliver this? Is it reminiscent of anything in my own life story? Draw up your own YESS plan to keep yourself safe. Self-care when working with people is so important.

3. Follow the advice in the 'Planning for teachers and PSHE leads' sections, within the lesson plans in Part III. No matter how well we know the young people we work with, we cannot be 100 per cent sure that something that comes up isn't reflected somewhere in their lives.

COMIC 1

ALLEN – THE STORY OF A YOUNG CARER

Content note: parent with a mental illness, bullying

COMIC 1   COMIC 2   COMIC 3   COMIC 4   COMIC 5   COMIC 6

COMIC 1   COMIC 2   COMIC 3   COMIC 4   COMIC 5   COMIC 6

COMIC 1   COMIC 2   COMIC 3   COMIC 4   COMIC 5   COMIC 6

COMIC 1   COMIC 2   COMIC 3   COMIC 4   COMIC 5   COMIC 6

COMIC 1   COMIC 2   COMIC 3   COMIC 4   COMIC 5   COMIC 6

COMIC 1   COMIC 2   COMIC 3   COMIC 4   COMIC 5   COMIC 6

COMIC 1   COMIC 2   COMIC 3   COMIC 4   COMIC 5   COMIC 6

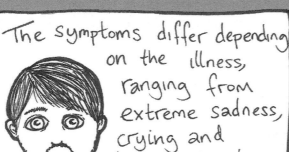

The symptoms differ depending on the illness, ranging from extreme sadness, crying and losing interest in life....

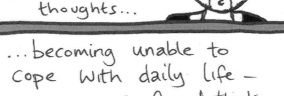

...to delusions and hallucinations - seeing and hearing things that aren't really there, paranoia, thinking people can hear their thoughts...

...becoming unable to cope with daily life – confused thinking. Not looking after themselves and people they care for.

They might start doing things that seem very out of character.

COMIC 1   COMIC 2   COMIC 3   COMIC 4   COMIC 5   COMIC 6

Mental illness can be managed with medication and therapy. If you are worried it is important that you talk to someone.

Sometimes it's difficult to talk.

We might bottle up our worries and difficult feelings, or try to pretend that they aren't there.

Why do you think we might do this?

What happens if you do this over a long period of time?

Write your answers in the bottle.

10

Regardless of mental health, we all have problems and worries. Your support circle is made up of people you trust and can talk to if you need to.
Try to name at least one person for each ring. (more if you can!)

1. NAN   2. TUTOR   3. YOUTH WORKERS

You can look after your own mental health by getting your 5-a-day.

mindapples = a day-to-day activity that is good for your mind.

What are your mindapples?

- SKATING
- MATES
- PLAYING DRUMS
- WALKING NAN'S DOG
- TAKING KIM TO THE PARK

Tweet to @mindapples

How could you be supportive to a friend who is showing signs of feeling down or stressed?

Caring for someone who has a long term illness or disability can be really tough.
If this affects you, there may be young carers services in your area. Ask someone or look online.

Whatever is going on for you, don't suffer in silence. These organisations are here to listen:

Childline: 0800 1111   **Samaritans**: 08457 909090

Get Connected: 0808 8084994

Mental health is as important as physical health. Look after yourself as well as each other.

12

COMIC 2

BRIAN – THE STORY OF A YOUNG PERSON WITH ADHD

1

COMIC 1 COMIC 2 COMIC 3 COMIC 4 COMIC 5 COMIC 6

Every day life can be a struggle for Brian. Being in trouble really gets to him.

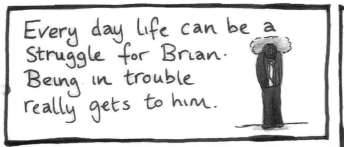

...but he loves his family...

...has some good mates...

...and he's brilliant at art.

One day he borrowed his dad's laptop to look on google for his art project.

He noticed something on google history...

Google™

A
ADHD
ADHD STATS
ADHD SUPPORT GROUP
PARENT SUPPORT GROUP

ADHD THE FACTS%
DEPRESSION
CRIME DRUGS
BAD

3

4

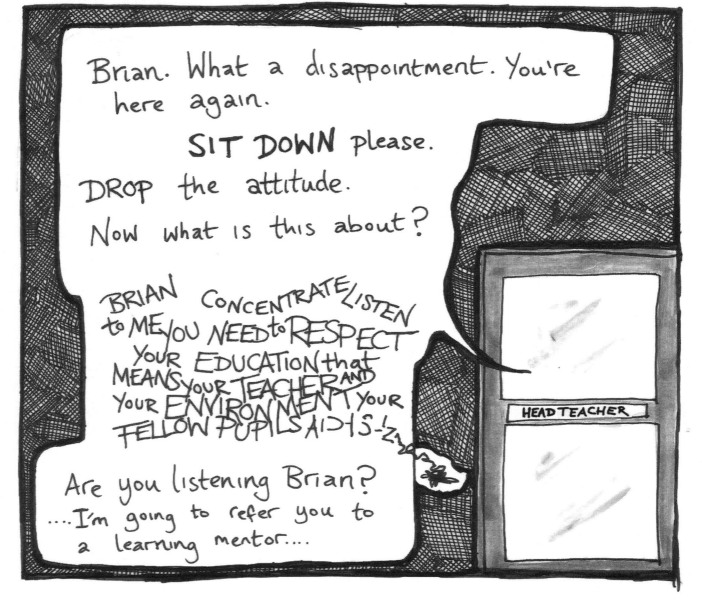

COMIC 1   COMIC 2   COMIC 3   COMIC 4   COMIC 5   COMIC 6

6

What does Brian need now from his new mentor?

Skills
(What can he do)

Qualities
(What is he like?)

COMIC 1 | COMIC 2 | COMIC 3 | COMIC 4 | COMIC 5 | COMIC 6

✓

What does Brian's mentor need to understand about Brian?

Brian's story

Brian's thoughts

Brian's feelings

Imagine Brian in 3 months' time.
How would we know if things had got better?

What could he start to do differently?

Who could help Brian?

They could be people already in his life, or others he could meet or speak to.

Brian's mentor decides to hold a 'Team Around the Child' meeting. A group of people who can help Brian get together with him and his family. They decide on a plan that everyone is involved in. What might that look like?

BRIAN'S PLAN

What can be done?	Who will do it?	How will it help?

I want Brian to be able to learn.

We want to be good mates.

We want him to be happy.

I want to help him to build on his strengths.

I want people to understand me.

COMIC 1   COMIC 2   COMIC 3   COMIC 4   COMIC 5   COMIC 6

He understands himself more now...

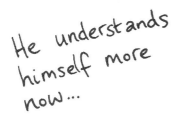

...He is SENSITIVE....

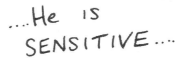

...Has loads of ENERGY...

...IS CREATIVE...

BRIAN HAS GOT

ADHD
(ATTENTION DEFICIT HYPERACTIVITY DISORDER)

...AND PERCEPTIVE

Brian has good days and bad days, (like we all do) but now he likes himself again – and that is important.

12

COMIC 3

EMILY – THE STORY OF A YOUNG PERSON EXPLORING HER SEXUAL IDENTITY

Content note: homophobia

1

2

COMIC 1   COMIC 2   COMIC 3   COMIC 4   COMIC 5   COMIC 6

COMIC 1   COMIC 2   COMIC 3   COMIC 4   COMIC 5   COMIC 6

COMIC 1 COMIC 2 COMIC 3 COMIC 4 COMIC 5 COMIC 6

7

COMIC 1   COMIC 2   COMIC 3   COMIC 4   COMIC 5   COMIC 6

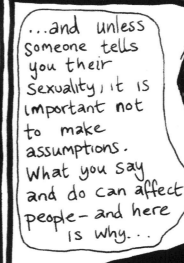

9

1938
2002
2014
1988
1885
2000
2003
1967
1992

* LGB history in England.

COMIC 1   COMIC 2   COMIC 3   COMIC 4   COMIC 5   COMIC 6

COMIC 1   COMIC 2   COMIC 3   COMIC 4   COMIC 5   COMIC 6

COMIC 4

JAY – THE STORY OF A YOUNG TRANSGENDER PERSON

Content note: transphobia, sexism, bullying

COMIC 1   COMIC 2   COMIC 3   **COMIC 4**   COMIC 5   COMIC 6

2

3

I watched a film about a male impersonator. She cut her hair and played male parts on stage in the 1890s.
That gave me an idea...

Can you make it as masculine as possible? I'm playing a boy in a production.

I changed the colour too and I donated the hair to charity.

IT FELT GREAT.

COMIC 1　　COMIC 2　　COMIC 3　　**COMIC 4**　　COMIC 5　　COMIC 6

I started clothes shopping in men's shops and I changed my name on Facebook to Jay instead of Jenny. Though technically I hadn't 'come out'.

6

We were brought together because we come under the umbrella of being transgender, but WE ARE ALL SO DIFFERENT ...and so are our experiences

I worry if I don't 'pass', I'm not trans enough

My teacher said 'Why can't you just be a lesbian?!'

I'm open about being trans and I go to the young equalities group

I'm moving schools because of bullying. Sometimes I self harm.

My parents are struggling with it but my nan gets it.

I don't see myself as male or female, but I know WHO I AM.

COMIC 1 · COMIC 2 · COMIC 3 · COMIC 4 · COMIC 5 · COMIC 6

COMIC 1   COMIC 2   COMIC 3   COMIC 4   COMIC 5   COMIC 6

I was assigned female but I am a heterosexual man.

I was assigned male but I am a gay woman.

I was assigned female but I am a man.

I was assigned male but I am a heterosexual woman.

Who is CIS and Who is TRANS?

CISGENDER

Is a word used to describe a person who identifies as the gender they were assigned at birth.

TRANSGENDER

Is a word used to describe a person who does not.

I was assigned female and I am a heterosexual woman.

I was assigned male and I am a gay man.

People assume I'm a boy but I don't always feel like one.

I'm not a boy or a girl.

I am just me.

COMIC 1   COMIC 2   COMIC 3   **COMIC 4**   COMIC 5   COMIC 6

COMIC 5

LAUREN – THE STORY OF A YOUNG PERSON WITH POST-TRAUMATIC STRESS DISORDER

Content note: being in care, abuse, violence, racism

1

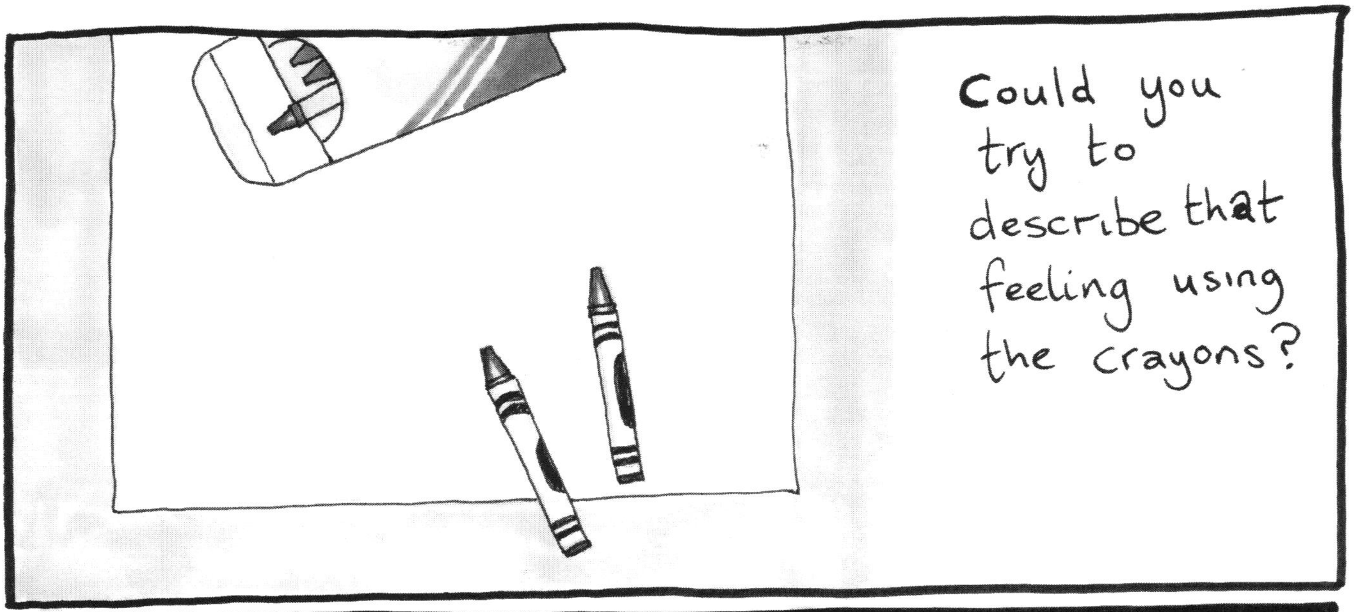
Could you try to describe that feeling using the crayons?

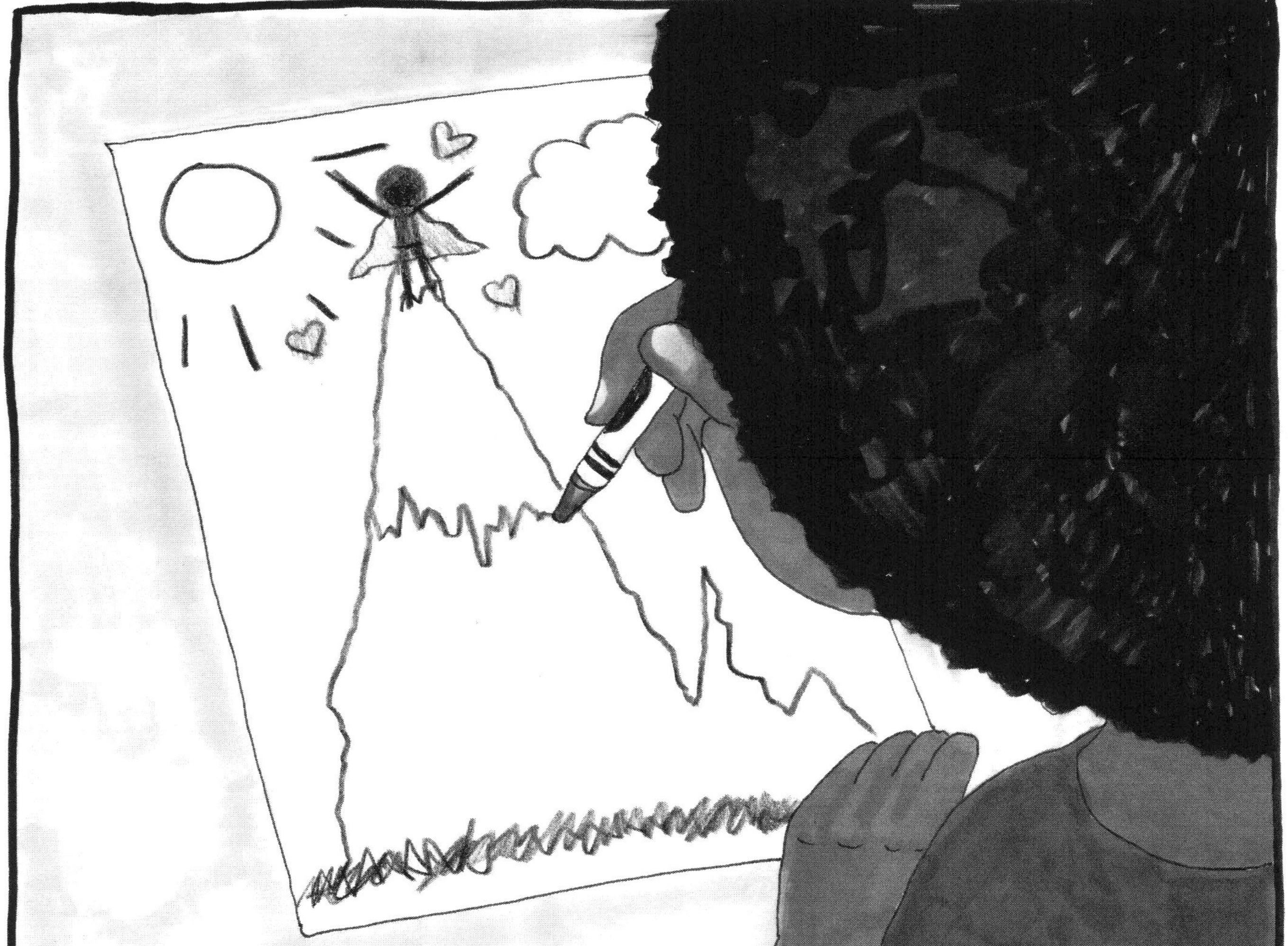

7

COMIC 1   COMIC 2   COMIC 3   COMIC 4   **COMIC 5**   COMIC 6

9

10

COMIC 1   COMIC 2   COMIC 3   COMIC 4   COMIC 5   COMIC 6

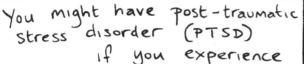

I thought I'd moved on, that the past was in the past. How am I supposed to help other people?

It takes time to recover from traumatic events in your life. This ISN'T a sign of weakness

You might have post-traumatic stress disorder (PTSD) if you experience things like flashbacks, nightmares, intense distress when you are reminded...

...you might feel depressed, or even that you don't have any feelings. Like you're numb.

FEELINGS

OFF

ON

...And anxiety, or always being on RED ALERT. Sometimes that can feel like hyperactivity.

12

13

It helps to understand how the brain works. A psychiatrist called Dan Siegel described a way of using your hand to imagine your brain...

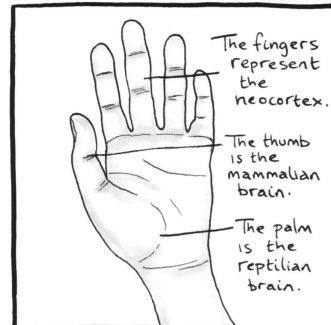

The fingers represent the neocortex.

The thumb is the mammalian brain.

The palm is the reptilian brain.

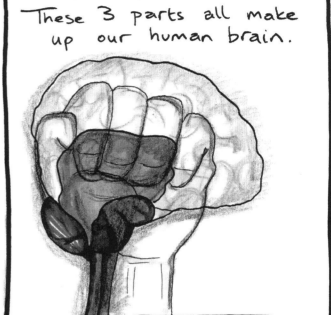

These 3 parts all make up our human brain.

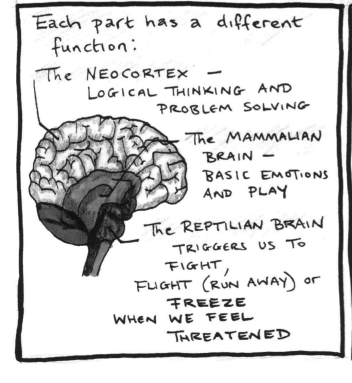

Each part has a different function:

The NEOCORTEX — LOGICAL THINKING AND PROBLEM SOLVING

The MAMMALIAN BRAIN — BASIC EMOTIONS AND PLAY

The REPTILIAN BRAIN TRIGGERS US TO FIGHT, FLIGHT (RUN AWAY) or FREEZE WHEN WE FEEL THREATENED

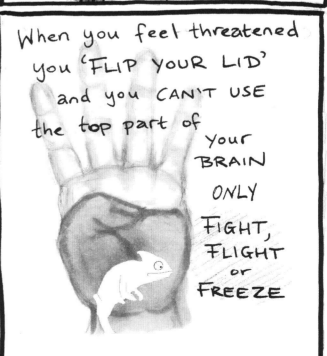

When you feel threatened you 'FLIP YOUR LID' and you CAN'T USE the top part of your BRAIN ONLY FIGHT, FLIGHT or FREEZE

14

When something in your environment triggers a traumatic memory or emotion, your brain can relive the trauma as if it is happening now.

The 'fight or flight' response evolved to protect us. Think about our ancestors....

If the surroundings are unfamiliar or unsafe

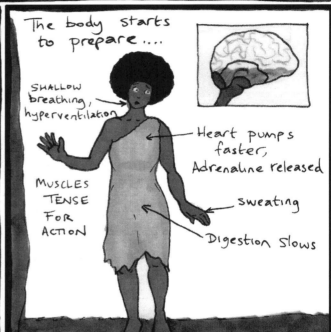

The body starts to prepare....

SHALLOW breathing, hyperventilation

Heart pumps faster, Adrenaline released

MUSCLES TENSE FOR ACTION

Sweating

Digestion slows

....for ATTACK. We don't have time to work out PROS and CONS - so the neocortex shuts off...

The ONLY WAY to switch it back on is via the mammalian brain. It knows we're safe when we play...

...or reconnect with those who care about us.

15

COMIC 1 COMIC 2 COMIC 3 COMIC 4 COMIC 5 COMIC 6

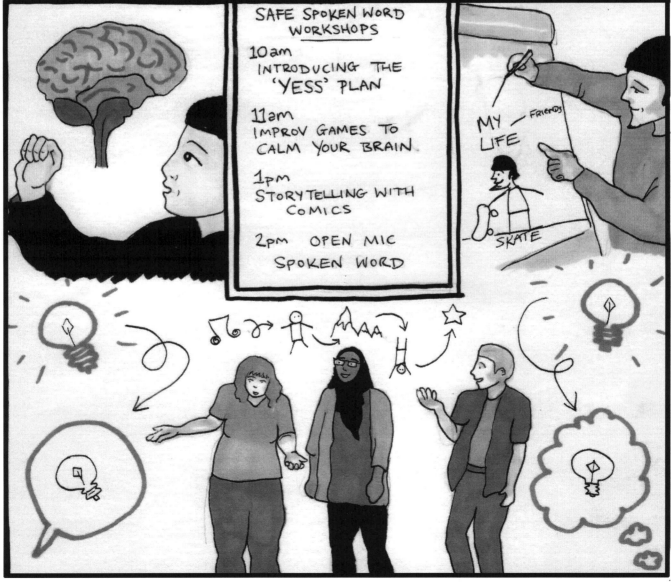

COMIC 1   COMIC 2   COMIC 3   COMIC 4   COMIC 5   COMIC 6

20

COMIC 1   COMIC 2   COMIC 3   COMIC 4   **COMIC 5**   COMIC 6

COMIC 6

CARTOON YOUR LIFE –
HOW TO MAKE A COMIC

COMIC 1 COMIC 2 COMIC 3 COMIC 4 COMIC 5 COMIC 6

Try it on THIS PAGE HERE

It seems weird at first, trying to draw your feelings. Sometimes it is difficult to even know what your feelings are. Start by remembering the last time you had each of these emotions, and then making shapes, marks and scribbles in the boxes.

ANGER

JOY

SHOCK

SADNESS

EXCITEMENT

CALM

If you want to, you could pick one and make a bigger image on a separate piece of paper - using crayons, paint, ink or ANYTHING ELSE you can find.

... and they can still DO all of the THINGS.

... they can MOVE:

(KEEP THE LIMBS ATTACHED TO THE CORNERS.)

... and make FACES:

Eyes half way down... Unless looking up... Or down... Side... to side

Happy   Sad   Shock   Angry   ?

Blank   Asleep   Weird   Grief   Robot or Something

And they can have feelings inside:

The MINDFUL doodle

MINDFULNESS means maintaining a moment-by-moment awareness of our thoughts, feelings, bodily sensations and surrounding environment

① Close your eyes and notice what is happening in your body.

② Breathe slowly and deeply for 1-3 minutes, not focussing on your thoughts, but letting them drift by.

③ Notice what is happening in your body again, before slowly opening your eyes.

④ DRAW whatever you noticed on the doodle person

⑤ What would they say if they had a voice?

7

See what you can do with these doodle people. Try different faces, movements and emotions:

And if you want to add words to your images, here are some ways you could do it.

AS FOR OBJECTS
they are all made out of shapes...

CIRCLE

SQUARE/
RECTANGLE

TRIANGLE

and forms...

 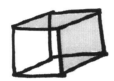 

This sort of thing takes practice but you can draw basic things with shapes:

TV

CHAIR

DOG?

DRUM

WEIRD GUITAR SORT OF THING

If there is more than one person in the picture you can make them look different by giving each of them a distinguishing feature

Some people like to use panels, some don't.

It can add structure

BEGINNING	MIDDLE	END

As well as doodle diaries, you can also make comics and zines with this style. Or any style you want in fact. Zines are like homemade magazines.

MAKE A MIND-MAP FOR IDEAS

THINGS I KNOW ABOUT

MY LIFE STORIES

What do I WANT TO SHARE WITH PEOPLE?

THINGS I CARE ABOUT

12

You can make an 8 page zine with one sheet of A4 or bigger. If it's A4 you can photocopy it and hand them out to friends and family.
PUT YOUR STORIES in their BRAINS.

Step ①

Fold paper into 8 equal parts

Step ②

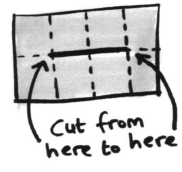

Cut from here to here

Step ③

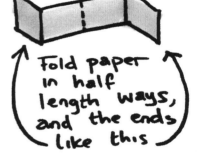

Fold paper in half length ways, and the ends like this

Step ④

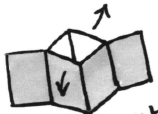

Pop centre out and away from each other

Draw on all the pages etc.

⑤

Unfold and photocopy – it only needs to be copied on one side!

And that is it!

PART III

PRACTICAL
RESOURCES

MIRRORING USING COMICS

A powerful method of communicating with young people is to use comics or stories as a mirror to echo their experiences from a safe distance. There are two examples here of comics I've created to explore peer pressure and anger. Each comic is only a page long, which means much of the narrative is like a blank canvas. We don't know the whole story, so we can imagine it and project onto the character and their world.

I find that young people will sometimes pick up on something that isn't obvious from the story but that is relevant to them personally. For example, when I showed the Callum story to Mike, he said he thought Callum was angry because he'd been arguing with his friends at the park. The comic doesn't mention arguments with friends in the park, but Mike was experiencing bullying in his local community, so this was his own projection.

When working with young people, you can draw your own short comic strips using fictional characters, or find comics pages in books that echo themes or dilemmas in that young person's life. There are graphic novels available covering so many issues, from domestic violence to mental health, and they can often be ordered at the library and pages photocopied. It can be especially powerful if you have the permission of a young person to share a comic they have made about their own experience, such as mental health, with another young person who is going through something similar.

Show the comic to the young person and try asking questions such as

- What do you think is going on in this story?

- What do you think the character is struggling with?

- What are they feeling?

- What do they need?

- What advice would you give him or her if they were a friend of yours?

This technique will give the young person an opportunity to explore the issue through a different perspective. It allows them to explore new solutions, ways of behaving, and alternative endings, without forcing them on the individual. By witnessing the story of another, whether fictional or otherwise, they are more likely to share their own.

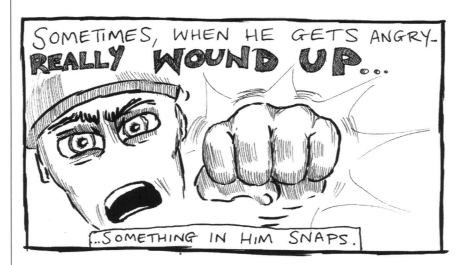

THE SAFE
SPOKEN WORD

A ONE-DAY WORKSHOP FOR YOUNG PEOPLE OR PROFESSIONALS ON HOW TO USE STORIES SAFELY

1. **Briefly introduce facilitators and opening round.**

   Each participant says their name, something about it, how they feel towards it, whether they would like a new name for the day. Explain that, if they want to experiment with being a different way to how they usually are, today they can.

2. **Group agreement.**

   Let people know they can sit with whoever they choose. Explain the purpose – to creatively share stories with each other in a safe way, whether that be through writing, drawing comics, poetry or song.

   - Make them aware that there may be issues or emotions that come up, and that the important thing about 'The Safe Spoken Word' is that it must be safe for everyone to feel included and able to share their stories if they choose to.

   - Explain the YESS plan and use it to come up with an agreement about how to make this space as safe as possible. Divide into smaller groups if necessary. Use large sheets of paper drawn up into quarters to represent the four sections of the YESS plan:

     » YOU: How are you feeling? What mood are you in? How tired or energetic are you? Has there been anything difficult going on in your life at the moment?

     » ENVIRONMENT: Does the space feel safe? Do you know anyone here? Can you expect people here to be kind to you and others in the room? Will the things that you say stay confidential?

     » STORY: The expression that something is 'triggering' means that the content of something that is read, seen or heard causes someone who has suffered a traumatic event to once again feel the emotions they felt during the time of their traumatic experience. It can be 'triggering' if someone shares experiences similar to those in the story, or to talk about difficult things that have happened to us.

» STRATEGY: If you do start to experience some strong emotions or start to feel numb, what can you do to look after yourself? Is there anything anyone here could do to help you?

Ask the group to use Post-it notes to come up with suggestions of ways that they can make the group safe for the day. Provide one example for each and explain your confidentiality policy:

YOU: Take the time to notice what is going on in your body and in your thoughts, and have quiet times during the day. Take occasional 'mindful minutes' that involve silent breathing and noticing how you are feeling.

ENVIRONMENT: Agree to be proactively kind to each other throughout the day, with small gestures – the way you talk to each other, or making an effort to include and listen to someone who isn't as confident as others. Does anything in the room need to be changed or moved around? Sometimes people feel better if they are sitting near a door, or if the chairs are arranged in a certain way. Do you understand the confidentiality policy?

STORY: Take some time to consider what you want to share and what you want to keep private for the day. Remember that you don't have to share everything.

STRATEGY: Agree on a 'buddy' for the day that you can talk to. If you feel unsafe you can let someone know, and leave the room if you need to. Go for a quick walk around the block. Arrange to do something to look after yourself once the day has finished.

3. Ask everyone to look at the 'Cartoon Your Life' worksheets (Comic 6).

Look at pages 1, 2 and 3. Write or draw non-stop for five minutes – include what you expect, how you feel about the day, and any other 'stuff' that is on your mind. Talk to the person next to you about what that was like. You don't have to tell them what you wrote.

4. Improv games.

Now that the group have 'arrived' individually, the purpose of these games is to start to feel comfortable around each other.

a. The whole group are going to create a story together. Stand in a circle. The first person starts by saying a word that will begin a story, accompanied with an action. The next person says the next word, until everyone has spoken and the story is complete. Then break into partners and do the same as a pair. Each time the facilitator gives the signal, swap partners.

b. The next game is about feedback. One person who is feeling ready to be the centre of attention volunteers to leave the room. While they are gone the group decide something that they want the person to do when they come back in. It could be anything – to jump up and down or to 'high five' a specific person – whatever the group decides. When they come back in they are told that the group has decided on something they want them to do, but the only hint they will get is by applause. The closer they get to doing the thing that was asked of them, the more the group applauds. When they do the thing correctly, everyone will jump up and give them high fives and praise. Afterwards feedback.

Questions to ask: Did the group expect them to succeed? How did the person feel when they were given applause? What was it like being the centre of attention? Did anything surprise you? Is there any learning we can take from this activity?

c. Now everyone who wants to can come and stand in front of the room in turn, and everyone will applaud them. Just for being there.

5. Drawing games (see 'Comic engagement' in Chapter 2 for full explanations of the activities).

a. Doodle Collaboration

b. One-Page Story

c. Make Your Mark

What was that like?

6. Read the 'Lauren' comic (Comic 5) and complete the activities from the Lauren lesson plan in the section that follows.

7. Individually continue with the remaining pages of the 'Cartoon Your Life' workbook (Comic 6).

8. Make it! Each person chooses whether to make an eight-page zine or a more detailed one page.

9. Show and Tell. Each person is invited to share their story. Remember the YESS plan and to be supportive of each other. Give the group encouragement, but people can opt out if they would prefer not to share. Invite others

to give each other supportive feedback – what did they enjoy or find interesting in each others' stories?

10. Feedback: ask them to draw or write their feedback about the day using the materials and blank pieces of paper rather than forms. Ask them what went well and to make suggestions for how the day can be run differently next time.

YOUNG CARERS LESSON PLAN: ALLEN'S STORY

Date:	School:	
Class:	Year group:	Key stage:
Number of pupils:	Number of pupils with additional needs:	

Lesson title: Cartooning Teen Stories: Young Carers

Intended learning outcomes

- To be made aware that children and young people may take on some of the responsibilities of caring for a family member, and how that might affect the life of that child.
- To consider the impact of bullying someone who is a young carer.
- To develop empathy and to begin to think about ways we can impact and support each others' mental health.
- To be aware that everyone has mental health needs, and to provide examples of ways that we can look after our minds.

Key messages

- Mental health is as important as physical health, and there are ways that we can care for our own or seek help when needed.
- It is ok to talk about mental health and ask for help.
- Young carers carry huge responsibility on top of day-to-day activities such as school, college or work.
- We should try not to make assumptions about other people's home lives or families, and bullying others is never an acceptable way to behave.
- If someone is affected by a mental health issue, consider how to be a good friend to that person.

Planning for teachers and PSHE leads

It is likely that there will be people in the room affected by some of the issues within this lesson. They may or may not feel able to communicate this to you or others in the room. Take the time to prepare pupils for this by:

- allowing them to sit with who they want to in this lesson. It is important that they feel safe

- making them aware that there may be issues within this lesson that affect them or someone they know

- telling them that if they are talking about someone, remember to keep their identity anonymous

- letting them know that it is ok if at any time they feel that they need to leave the classroom, and just to let someone know

- telling them that if they need to talk to someone about any of the issues in this lesson, they can come to you or specific named staff, such as the school nurse.

Don't choose specific pupils to read aloud. This may be too personal for some.

Take the time to find out where to signpost if pupils ask. There may be a Young Carers Service in your local area that you can refer to.

Teaching/learning activities

1. It is likely that there will be people in the room affected by some of the issues within this lesson. Begin with ground rules including the above advice.

2. Ask the class – what is your understanding of a) a young carer b) mental health and c) mental illness.

3. In pairs, complete the Young Carers quiz, followed by a whole class discussion.

4. Read the 'Allen' comic.

5. Group discussion: Did you learn anything from the story? Was there anything that surprised you? Remind the class that this comic provides only ONE example of one person's story – it is not representative of all young carers.

6. Post-it note activity: Have big sheets of paper around the room with one of the below questions on each. Give pupils pads of Post-it notes and invite them to write their answers on the sticky notes. They can stick them to the paper if they want them to be included. This is OPTIONAL – it is important that pupils feel safe enough to opt out, opt in or remain anonymous depending on how emotionally 'safe' this subject is for them to talk about. When finished, read out some or all of the answers and ask if anyone has any comments. Use your facilitation skills to encourage or challenge where you feel necessary.

   - Why do you think the girls in the comic bullied Allen?
   - Why do you think Allen kept the bullying to himself?
   - If you were Allen's friend, how could you help him?

7. Individually fill in the connected worksheets and discuss in pairs.

8. Signposting and debrief: What one thing have you learned today that you could use in your life? Give out a list of services or people they can go to for support.

Further information/signposting

Make yourself aware of Carers Services in your local area and local Youth Support Services.

Young Minds: www.youngminds.org.uk

Rethink Mental Illness: www.rethink.org

Definitions

Young Carer: Young carers are children and young people who take on practical and/or emotional caring responsibilities within the home that would normally be expected of an adult. This comic provides only ONE example of one person's story – it is not representative of all young carers.

Mental Health: A person's psychological and emotional well-being.

Mental Illness: A condition which causes serious disorder in a person's behaviour or thinking.

Allen worksheet 1

Sometimes it's difficult to talk.

We might bottle up our feelings or try to pretend they aren't there. Why do you think we do this?

What happens if you do this over a long period of time?

Write your answers in the bottle.

We can't make feelings that we don't want to have disappear, so how can we let them out gently?

Allen worksheet 2

Your support circle is made up of people you trust and can talk to if you need to. Try to name at least one person for each ring.

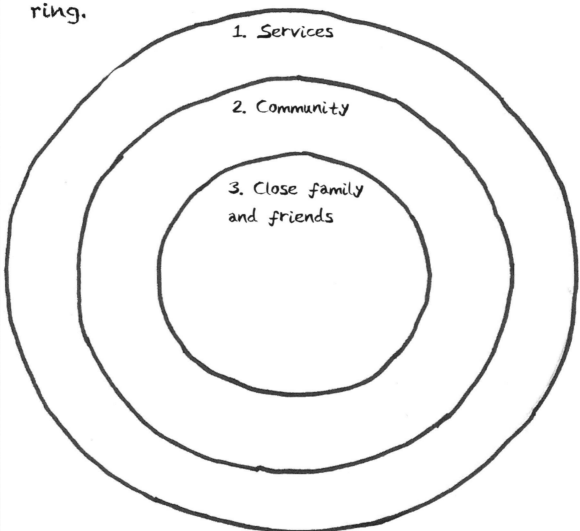

Services might be youth services, counsellors, your doctor or any professional whose job it is to help you.

Community can mean different things to different people, but it could be people in your school, religious group or community centre.

Allen worksheet 3

Mindapples = a day-to-day activity that is good for your mind.

This could be anything that makes you feel better. Research has shown that the things that keep us mentally healthy are things that help us to:

- Connect with others
- Be active
- Take notice of the world around us
- Learn something new
- Give to others

What are yours?

_____

_____

_____

_____

_____

Young Carers: Quiz

1. According to the 2011 census how many young people under the age of 18 are providing care?

   - 109,363

   - 130,363

   - 166,363

2. According to the LSYPE how many young carers are caring for someone who has a mental illness?

   - 11%

   - 23%

   - 29%

   - 33%

3. The 2011 census tells us what percentage of young carers (based on those under 18) are aged 5-7 years old?

   - 1%

   - 4%

   - 6%

Young Carers: Quiz (Cont.)

4. According to the 2011 census what is the average age of a young carer?

   - 10-14

   - 15

   - 16-17

5. Which of the following tasks may a young carer do?

   - Helping someone to wash, dress or go to the toilet

   - Cleaning, cooking and helping someone to eat

   - Shopping, paying bills and sorting out household finances

   - Administering medicine

   - Providing emotional support and company

   - Helping someone to move around

   - Looking for early warning signs of deterioration

Young Carers: Quiz (Cont.)

6. Which of the following are difficulties a young carer may face?

- Absence and lateness

- Tiredness, resulting in a loss of concentration

- Difficulty in joining extra curricular activities

- Maintaining a social life with their friends

- Difficulties completing homework and coursework on time

- Anxiety

- Isolation

- Feelings of anger and frustration

- Lack of confidence and self esteem

- Back or neck pain due to lifting

- Need to have mobile phone in school

- Cares for peers

- Has a lot of knowledge about illnesses and disabilities

- Can have a false sense of maturity

ADHD LESSON PLAN: BRIAN'S STORY

Date:	School:	
Class:	Year group:	Key stage:
Number of pupils:	Number of pupils with additional needs:	

Lesson title: Cartooning Teen Stories: ADHD

Intended learning outcomes

- To educate pupils about the myths and facts about ADHD.
- To consider why some pupils benefit from extra support.
- To apply solution-focussed planning to their own lives.

Key messages

- It is not always known to others in the class that someone has additional needs.
- Conditions such as ADHD can make life harder but there are also traits that can be recognised as strengths.

Planning for teachers and PSHE leads

It is likely that there will be people in the room affected by some of the issues within this lesson. They may or may not feel able to communicate this to you or others in the room. Take the time to prepare pupils for this by:

- making them aware that there may be issues within this lesson that affect them or someone they know

- telling them that if they are talking about someone, remember to keep their identity anonymous

- letting them know that it is ok if at any time they feel that they need to leave the classroom, and just to let someone know

- telling them that if they need to talk to someone about any of the issues in this lesson, they can come to you or specific named staff, such as the school nurse.

Don't choose specific pupils to read aloud. It may be too personal for some.

Take the time to find out where to signpost if pupils ask. There will be local services that you can refer to. If somebody thinks they may have ADHD they should see their doctor.

Teaching/learning activities

1. It is likely that there will be people in the room affected by some of the issues within this lesson. Include ground rules and above advice.

2. ADHD quiz – True or False? (whole class).

3. Read the 'Brian' comic.

4. Discuss: Did you learn anything? Did anything surprise you?

5. Complete 'Brian' worksheets.

6. In pairs, discuss whether you could apply any of these tools to your own life. Choose one of the tools and write or draw it about yourself. For example:

   - What skills and qualities would you look for in a person who was supporting you?

   - What do people need to understand about a) your story, b) your thoughts and c) your feelings, in order to be able to help you?

   - Imagine your life in three months' time – how would you know if things had got better? What could you start to do differently?

   - Create a visual map of your 'team' of support. This could include services, school and community, friends and family.

7. Signposting: Where to go if you need help with any of these issues – include any local mentoring services that accept self-referrals or that you could refer to.

Further information/signposting

Find out about local mentoring/youth support services including Child and Adolescent Mental Health Services and what their referral processes are.

Young Minds: www.youngminds.org.uk

ADHD Foundation: www.adhdfoundation.org.uk

Definitions

This comic provides only one person's experience of ADHD. It is not representative of all people who have ADHD.

Attention Deficit Hyperactivity Disorder (ADHD): A group of behavioural symptoms that include inattentiveness, hyperactivity and impulsiveness. Common symptoms of ADHD include: a short attention span or being easily distracted, restlessness, constant fidgeting or overactivity, being impulsive. These can also be symptoms of something other than ADHD, such as trauma, and need formal diagnosis from a health professional.

1. Inattentive

This is what is typically referred to when someone uses the term ADD rather than ADHD. This means a person shows enough symptoms of inattention (or easy distractibility) but isn't hyperactive or impulsive.

2. Hyperactive-Impulsive

This type occurs when a person has symptoms of hyperactivity and impulsivity but not inattention.

3. Combined

This type is when a person has symptoms of inattention, hyperactivity and impulsivity.

Additional Educational Needs (AEN): A learning, language, emotional, behavioural or physical difficulty or need, leading to significantly greater difficulty in accessing learning than the majority of students of the same age.

ADHD: True or False?

1. ADHD stands for Attention Deficit Hyperactivity Disorder.

TRUE or FALSE

2. ADHD is not a real disorder, it is a label given to naughty children.

TRUE or FALSE

3. ADHD only affects boys.

TRUE or FALSE

4. ADHD is the result of bad parenting.

TRUE or FALSE

5. People with ADHD have below average intelligence.

TRUE or FALSE

LGBT ISSUES AND HOMOPHOBIA
LESSON PLAN: EMILY'S STORY

Date:	School:	
Class:	Year group:	Key stage:
Number of pupils:	Number of pupils with additional needs:	

Lesson title: Cartooning Teen Stories: LGB issues and homophobia

Intended learning outcomes

Note: This lesson plan does not cover any trans issues, despite occasionally using the abbreviation LGBT. This is because gender and sexuality are two different subjects; however, LGBT is often the term used as an umbrella term. This is not to ignore 'T' issues – there is a separate lesson for 'T' – see 'Jay's Story'.

- To understand what LGBT stands for.
- To gain some knowledge of LGB history and how relevant laws have shaped society.
- To explore how emerging feelings regarding sexuality can affect the relationships we form with others.

Key messages

- Homophobia and heterosexism doesn't only affect LGBT people, it creates inequality generally.
- It is ok to experience sexuality in different ways, whether that be identifying as lesbian, gay, bisexual or any other label such as pansexual or asexual. It is equally ok not to label your sexuality at all, or not to be sure.
- It is important to notice your own prejudice, to question it, and not to make assumptions regarding other people's sexuality.

Planning for teachers and PSHE leads

It is likely that there will be people in the room affected by some of the issues within this lesson. They may or may not feel able to communicate this to you or others in the room. Take the time to prepare pupils for this by:

- making them aware that there may be issues within this lesson that affect them or someone they know

- telling them that if they are talking about someone, remember to keep their identity anonymous

- letting them know that it is ok if at any time they feel that they need to leave the classroom, and just to let someone know

- telling them that if they need to talk to someone about any of the issues in this lesson, they can come to you or specific named staff, such as the school nurse.

Don't choose specific pupils to read aloud. This may be too personal for some.

Take the time to find out where to signpost if pupils ask. There may be LGBT Services in your local area that you can refer to.

Teaching/learning activities

1. It is likely that there will be people in the room affected by some of the issues within this lesson. Begin with ground rules including the above advice.

2. LGB history quiz.

3. Read the 'Emily' comic.

4. Discussion:

   - What are the key messages?

   - What does LGBT stand for?

5. Post-it note activity: Have big sheets of paper around the room with one of the below questions on each. Give pupils pads of Post-it notes and invite them to write their answers on the sticky notes. They can stick them to the paper if they want them to be included. This is OPTIONAL – it is important that pupils feel safe enough to opt out, opt in or remain anonymous depending on how emotionally 'safe' this subject is for them to talk about. When finished, read out some or all of the answers and ask if anyone has any comments. Use your facilitation skills to encourage or challenge where you feel necessary.

   - Can you give one example of direct homophobia and one example of indirect homophobia?

   - Can you think of five examples of common gender stereotyping such as 'pink is a girl's colour'?

   - How might these stereotypes affect people?

   - How could you challenge stereotyping or homophobia?

6. Support/signposting (see below).

Further information/signposting

Identify staff within the school that pupils can go to to talk about these issues. Is there an anonymous way to report prejudice-based bullying? What are the services for LGBT people in your local area?

Stonewall: www.stonewall.org.uk

Definitions

LGBT+: Any combination of letters attempting to represent identities – this one represents Lesbian, Gay, Bisexual, Transgender.

Asexual: A person who generally does not experience sexual attraction (or very little) to any group of people.

Bisexual: A person who experiences sexual, romantic, physical and/or spiritual attraction to people of their own gender as well as another gender.

Coming Out: The process of revealing your sexuality or gender identity to individuals in your life.

Gay: A term used to describe somebody who is attracted to the same gender as themselves.

Heterosexism: Behaviour that assumes preferential treatment to heterosexual people.

Heterosexual: A medical definition for a person who is attracted to someone with the other gender (or, literally, biological sex) than they have.

Homophobia: Fear, anger, intolerance, resentment or discomfort with LGB people.

Pansexual: A person who experiences sexual, romantic, physical and/or spiritual attraction to members of all gender identities/expressions.

Questioning: The process of exploring one's own sexual orientation.

See more at: http://itspronouncedmetrosexual.com

GENDER IDENTITY LESSON PLAN: JAY'S STORY

Date:	School:	
Class:	Year group:	Key stage:
Number of pupils:	Number of pupils with additional needs:	

Lesson title: Cartooning Teen Stories: Gender

Intended learning outcomes

- To understand transgender and cisgender as umbrella terms, and to understand the ways in which people experience gender differently.
- To recognise the ways in which gender stereotypes are oppressive.
- To learn what is respectful behaviour and what is not towards people who are transgender.
- To identify ways of challenging sexism and transphobia.

Key messages

- Gender stereotypes place limitations on people. Every person should be free from social limitations pertaining to gender, without discrimination, and without verbal or physical abuse.
- There is still much work to be done in the form of changing attitudes and the currently gendered way of thinking, and each of us have the opportunity to make a difference, no matter how small.

Planning for teachers and PSHE leads

Take time to educate yourself about gender issues before conducting this lesson. If you are unfamiliar with the topic it will be difficult to facilitate a useful discussion, as there are potential areas for confusion such as the difference between sexuality and gender identity.

It is likely that there will be people in the room affected by some of the issues within this lesson. They may or may not feel able to communicate this to you or others in the room. Take the time to prepare pupils for this by:

- allowing them to sit with who they choose. It is important that they feel safe

- making them aware that there may be issues within this lesson that affect them or someone they know

- telling them that if they are talking about someone, remember to keep their identity anonymous

- letting them know that it is ok if at any time they feel that they need to leave the classroom, and just to let someone know

- telling them that if they need to talk to someone about any of the issues in this lesson, they can come to you or specific named staff, such as the school nurse.

Don't choose specific pupils to read aloud. This may be too personal for some.

Take the time to find out where to signpost if pupils ask. There may be LGBT Services in your local area that you can refer to.

Teaching/learning activities

- It is likely that there will be people in the room affected by some of the issues within this lesson. Include ground rules and the above advice.

- Ask the class, 'Does anyone know what transgender means?'

- Read the 'Jay' comic.

- Post-it note activity: Have a big sheet of paper divided in half with 'masculine' written on one side and 'feminine' on the other. What comes to mind when you think of these characteristics? Give pupils pads of Post-it notes and invite them to write their answers on the sticky notes. They can stick them to the paper if they want them to be included – this is OPTIONAL. When finished, read out some or all of the answers and ask if anyone has any comments. Explain that these perceptions of one's gender are social constructions. For example, a boy can enjoy ballet, but society may have different expectations over which activities are for boys and which are for girls. Can they think of anyone famous who has challenged gender stereotypes by not subscribing to an expected gender role?

- In small groups or pairs, complete the worksheets that go with the 'Jay' comic. Spend some time discussing the difference between sexuality and gender identity. For example, one character explains that she was 'assigned male but is a gay woman'. What does that mean? (She was assigned male, she identifies as female and she is attracted to women.)

- Have a class discussion about the pros and cons of getting information online. How do you think Jay kept himself safe when forming his support networks online? What other ways can you form support networks and get information, apart from online?

- Finally, explain that someone's trans identity is only a part of themselves, and many other things make up a person – their interests, hobbies and who they are as a person.

- Support/signposting (see below).

Further information/signposting

Find out about local LGBT services and give pupils the name of a school staff member they can go to for support regarding gender.

Mermaids: www.mermaidsuk.org.uk

Gendered Intelligence: http://genderedintelligence.co.uk

Definitions

LGBT+: Any combination of letters attempting to represent identities – this one represents Lesbian, Gay, Bisexual, Transgender.

Androgyny: A gender expression that has elements of both masculinity and femininity.

Bigender: A person who fluctuates between traditionally 'woman' and 'man' gender-based behaviour and identities, identifying with both genders (and sometimes a third gender).

Binary Gender: A traditional and outdated view of gender, limiting possibilities to 'man' and 'woman'.

Assigned Sex/Biological Sex: The physical anatomy and gendered hormones one is born with, generally described as male, female or intersex.

Cisgender: A description for a person whose gender identity, gender expression and biological sex all align (e.g. man, masculine and male).

Gender Expression: The external display of gender, through a combination of dress, demeanour, social behaviour and other factors.

Gender Identity: The internal perception of an individual's gender, and how they label themselves.

Genderless: A person who does not identify with any gender.

Intersex: A person with a set of sexual anatomy that doesn't fit within the labels of female or male.

Pansexual: A person who experiences attraction to members of all gender identities/expressions.

Sexuality: Who a person is romantically or sexually attracted to, if anyone.

Transgender: An umbrella term used to describe all people who are not cisgender.

Transitioning: A term used to describe the process of moving from one sex/ gender to another – sometimes this is done by hormone or surgical treatments.

Transsexual: A person whose gender identity is the binary opposite of their biological sex, who may undergo medical treatments to change their biological sex to align it with their gender identity.

Transvestite: A person who dresses as the binary opposite gender expression ('cross-dresses').

See more at: http://itspronouncedmetrosexual.com

Jay worksheet 1

Gender: Definitions

Use your own words to fill in the boxes to describe what each of these terms mean.

Jay worksheet 2

Think of things that you could do to challenge gender stereotypes and transphobia.

Write them in the speech bubbles.

TRAUMA AND RESILIENCE LESSON PLAN: LAUREN'S STORY

Date:	School:	
Class:	Year group:	Key stage:
Number of pupils:	Number of pupils with additional needs:	

Lesson title: Cartooning Teen Stories: Trauma and Resilience

Intended learning outcomes

- To understand why some people experience panic attacks and how to create emotionally safe spaces.

- To be aware of Post-Traumatic Stress Disorder, trauma and building resilience.

- To understand the 'Triune Brain' – and the elements of the reptilian brain, the mammalian brain and the neocortex and how they work together.

- To understand the benefits and risks of sharing personal stories, and how to protect yourself by introducing the YESS method of planning.

Key messages

- Trauma and resilience are not indicators of weakness and strength. Anyone can experience trauma and different levels of resilience depending on a number of influencing factors based on the experience, personal history, the environment and surrounding support.

- Levels of resilience can go up and down in different circumstances.

- Understanding the narrative of our life scripts and how the brain works can help us to plan coping strategies.

Planning for teachers and PSHE leads

The expression that something is 'triggering' means that content of something that is read, seen, heard, etc. causes someone who has suffered a traumatic event to once again feel the emotions they felt during the time of their traumatic experience. This particular lesson can be 'triggering' if someone has experiences similar to those in the story. Trigger warnings are designed to prevent unaware encountering of certain materials or subjects for the benefit of people who have an extremely strong and damaging emotional response (for example, post-traumatic flashbacks or urges to harm themselves) to such topics. Having these responses is called 'being triggered'. Be very sensitive with the planning of this session and the individual needs within the class. It is recommended that this lesson is used with Year 10 upwards. Be aware of Child Protection procedures within the school and be prepared in case of disclosure.

It is likely that there will be people in the room affected by some of the issues within this lesson. They may or may not feel able to communicate this to you or others in the room. Take the time to prepare pupils for this by:

- giving them the choice of where they sit and who they work with
- making them aware that there may be issues within this lesson that affect them or someone they know
- telling them that if they are talking about someone, remember to keep their identity anonymous
- letting them know that it is ok if at any time they feel that they need to leave the classroom, and just to let someone know
- telling them that if they need to talk to someone about any of the issues in this lesson, they can come to you or specific named staff, such as the school nurse.

Don't choose specific pupils to read aloud. This may be too personal for some.

Take the time to find out where to signpost or refer if needed. There will be services in your local area that you can refer to such as the Child and Adolescent Mental Health Services.

Teaching/learning activities

1. It is likely that there will be people in the room affected by some of the issues within this lesson. Include ground rules, the above advice and explain what a 'trigger warning' is and how it is applicable to this lesson.

2. Read the 'Lauren' comic.

3. Post-it note activity: Have big sheets of paper around the room with one of the below questions on each. Give pupils pads of Post-it notes and invite them to write their answers on the sticky notes. They can stick them to the paper if they want them to be included – this is OPTIONAL. When finished, read out some or all of the answers and ask if anyone has any comments.

   • What is trauma?

   • What is resilience?

   • What is Post-Traumatic Stress Disorder?

4. Group activity: On a large piece of paper draw a diagram of the brain and fill it with words and pictures to describe each of the three functions. For example: The reptilian brain could have a picture that represent fight, flight and freeze. The mammalian brain could include words about playing and connecting, and the neocortex could include images that represent logic and reasoning.

5. Small group discussions: Why is it important to share stories and how can you do it safely? Look at the YESS plan and discuss how it could be used.

6. Individual activity: Draw an example of your 'safe space'. This can be real or imagined. For example, a location of a favourite holiday, with or without other people or animals you feel safe with.

7. Support/signposting (see below).

Further information/signposting

Find out about local services such as Child and Adolescent Mental Health Services and any accessible counselling. Also reiterate key members of staff or others they can talk to such as the school nurse.

Mind: www.mind.org.uk

Young Minds: www.youngminds.org.uk

Childline: www.childline.org.uk

Definitions

Post-Traumatic Stress Disorder (PTSD): A mental health condition that's triggered by a traumatic event – either experiencing it or witnessing it. Symptoms may include flashbacks, nightmares and severe anxiety, as well as uncontrollable thoughts about the event.

Resilience: The capacity to withstand stress and catastrophe. People experience resilience differently at different times and in different contexts, depending on their own mental health at the time (You), the Environment that they are in, particular triggers in their life Stories and whether they have a Strategy for self-care (YESS).

Trauma: A deeply distressing or disturbing experience. This comic provides only one example – many situations can be experienced as traumatic. Other examples may include being in or being witness to an accident, abuse, violence, the sudden loss of a close family member or friend (death or otherwise). There are many others.

ANSWERS TO QUIZZES

YOUNG CARERS QUIZ

1. 166,363
2. 29%
3. 6%
4. 10–14
5. All
6. All

ADHD QUIZ

1. True
2. False
3. False
4. False
5. False

LGB QUIZ

Starting from the bottom of the page:

1. 1885
2. 1938
3. 1967
4. 1988
5. 1992
6. 2000
7. 2002
8. 2003
9. 2014

REFERENCES

Angelou, M. (1984) *I Know Why The Caged Bird Sings.* London: Virago.

Berne, E. (1961) *Transactional Analysis in Psychotherapy.* New York, NY: Grove Press.

Comics Magazine Association of America (1959) *Facts about Code-Approved Comics Magazines.* New York, NY: The Association.

Freud, S. (1909) *Analysis of a Phobia in a Five-Year-Old Boy.* The Standard Edition of the Complete Psychological Works of Sigmund Freud, Volume X: Two Case Histories ('Little Hans' and the 'Rat Man').

Green, K. (2013) *Lighter than My Shadow.* London: Jonathan Cape.

McCloud, S. (1993) *Understanding Comics: The Invisible Art.* New York, NY: HarperCollins Publishers.

McCloud, S. (2000) *Reinventing Comics.* New York, NY: HarperCollins Publishers.

Mindapples: Love Your Mind. Available at http://mindapples.org, accessed on 22 August 2015.

Oxford Health NHS Foundation Trust (2015) *Healthcare Services for Children and Young People.* Available at www.oxfordhealth.nhs.uk/children-and-young-people, accessed on 22 August 2015.

Perls, F. (1969) *Ego, Hunger, and Aggression: The Beginning of Gestalt Therapy.* New York, NY: Random House.

Siegel, D. (2011) *Dr. Dan Siegel's Hand Model.* Available at www.drdansiegel.com/resources/everyday_mindsight_tools, accessed on 22 August 2015.

Spiegelman, A. (1986) *Maus: A Survivor's Tale.* New York, NY: Pantheon.

Spiegelman, A. (2015) *What the…happened to comics.* Talk, 26 January 2015. Koffler Centre of the Arts.

Streeten, N. (2011) *Billy, Me and You: A Memoir of Grief and Recovery.* Brighton: Myriad Editions.

Williams, I. (2007) *Graphic Medicine.* Available at www.graphicmedicine.org, accessed on 22 August 2015.